P9-BZS-046

The History of Rap and Hip-Hop

THE MUSIC LIBRARY

The History of Rap and Hip-Hop

Soren Baker

LUCENT BOOKS

A part of Gale, Cengage Learning

GALE
CENGAGE Learning

Detroit • New York • San Francisco • New Haven, Conn • Waterville, Maine • London

GALE
CENGAGE Learning

LIBRARY OF CONGRESS CATALOGING-IN-PUBLICATION DATA

Baker, Soren, 1975-
    The history of rap and hip-hop / by Soren Baker.
        pages cm -- (The music library)
    Includes bibliographical references and index.
    ISBN 978-1-4205-0822-2 (hardcover)
    1. Rap (Music)--History and criticism--Juvenile literature. 2. Hip-hop--United States--Juvenile literature. I. Title.
    ML3531.B365 2012
    782.42164909--dc23
                        2012002278

Lucent Books
27500 Drake Rd.
Farmington Hills, MI 48331

ISBN-13: 978-1-4205-0822-2
ISBN-10: 1-4205-0822-9

Printed in the United States of America
1 2 3 4 5 6 7 16 15 14 13 12

CONTENTS

FOREWORD

In the nineteenth century, English novelist Charles Kingsley wrote, "Music speaks straight to our hearts and spirits, to the very core and root of our souls. . . . Music soothes us, stirs us up . . . melts us to tears." As Kingsley stated, music is much more than just a pleasant arrangement of sounds. It is the resonance of emotion, a joyful noise, a human endeavor that can soothe the spirit or excite the soul. Musicians can also imitate the expressive palette of the earth, from the violent fury of a hurricane to the gentle flow of a babbling brook.

The word *music* is derived from the fabled Greek muses, the children of Apollo who ruled the realms of inspiration and imagination. Composers have long called upon the muses for help and insight. Music is not merely the result of emotions and pleasurable sensations, however.

Music is a discipline subject to formal study and analysis. It involves the juxtaposition of creative elements such as rhythm, melody, and harmony with intellectual aspects of composition, theory, and instrumentation. Like painters mixing red, blue, and yellow into thousands of colors, musicians blend these various elements to create classical symphonies, jazz improvisations, country ballads, and rock-and-roll tunes.

Throughout centuries of musical history, individual musical elements have been blended and modified in infinite ways. The resulting sounds may convey a whole range of moods, emotions, reactions, and messages. Music, then, is both an expression and reflection of human experience and emotion.

The foundations of modern musical styles were laid down by the first ancient musicians who used wood, rocks, animal skins—and their own bodies—to re-create the sounds of the natural world in which they lived. With their hands, their feet, and their very breath they ignited the passions of listeners and moved them to their feet. The dancing, in turn, had a mesmerizing and hypnotic effect that allowed people to transcend their worldly concerns. Through music they could achieve a level of shared experience that could not be found in other forms of communication. For this reason, music has always been part of religious endeavors, from ancient Egyptian spiritual ceremonies to modern Christian masses. And it has inspired dance movements from kings and queens spinning the minuet to punk rockers slamming together in a mosh pit.

By examining musical genres ranging from Western classical music to rock and roll, readers will find a new understanding of old music and develop an appreciation for new sounds. Books in Lucent's Music Library focus on the music, the musicians, the instruments, and on music's place in cultural history. The songs and artists examined may be easily found in the CD and sheet music collections of local libraries so that readers may study and enjoy the music covered in the books. Informative sidebars, annotated bibliographies, and complete indexes highlight the text in each volume and provide young readers with many opportunities for further discussion and research.

Hip-Hop Culture

In the past thirty years, hip-hop culture has grown from its humble beginnings in the South Bronx section of New York City into a significant and influential cultural movement. Created in the mid-1970s by poor Bronx residents with few resources, hip-hop has become a billion-dollar industry whose reach now stretches around the world. Hip-hop has influenced the way people make music, the way they dance, and the way they wear their clothes. It has also shaped people's political views and turned many people into entrepreneurs.

Hip-hop culture encompasses four main components: rapping, DJing (disc jockeying), graffiti art, and B-boying (break dancing). At its inception, hip-hop was inspired by a variety of other art forms, many of which still influence and inspire hip-hop artists today. One of hip-hop's key characteristics is its ability to take an idea, a practice, or a way of doing something and make it into something new. For instance, spoken-word poets such as the Last Poets, Gil Scott-Heron, and Rudy Ray Moore, artists who recited rhyming lyrics over a musical backing, inspired rappers. Early hip-hop DJs invented a new way to enjoy music by repeating song passages best suited for dancing, while graffiti artists went from writing their names on buildings and billboards to creating dazzling art showcased in galleries. B-boys, also known as boogie boys or break-dancers, created a new style of dance featuring acrobatic skills.

Rap Takes Control

The most popular component of hip-hop culture is rap. Even though the words *hip-hop* and *rap* are often used interchangeably, they are not the same thing. Rap is part of a larger culture, while hip-hop is the culture itself. When people refer to hip-hop music, they typically mean rap, even though hip-hop music also includes other musical genres, such as rhythm and blues (R&B), soul, funk, jazz, and even rock and roll.

The first major rap recording was "Rapper's Delight," released in 1979 by the Sugarhill Gang. Just five years later, rap music was the dominant part of hip-hop culture. In early rap recordings, rappers typically performed over music made by musicians who simply copied the original music of other artists. By the mid-1980s, however, sampling

Spoken word artists the Last Poets—Jalal Mansur Nuriddin, Abiodun Oyewole, and Umar Bin Hassa (left to right), seen here in 1971—inspired early rappers.

and advances in technology and studio equipment (most significantly drum machines) changed the way rap was made. Sampling allowed producers, the people in rap who make the music, to incorporate segments of the original recordings of other artists into the producers' own material. Today, rap is made in a number of ways, including sampling and playing live music.

The way in which people rap has also evolved. Rappers in the 1970s favored a simple, straightforward style. The lyrics of most early rap songs focused on having a good time and boasted about the ability of a DJ or the lyrical prowess of the rapper. By the mid-1980s, known as the golden era of rap, rappers had developed complex deliveries and a number of rhyme styles to complement the explosion in sounds and kinds of music being produced. In the 1990s rap became largely regional, with New York rappers focusing on lyricism; Los Angeles, California, rappers focusing on gangster (or "gangsta") themes; and Southern artists boasting of their heritage. Today rappers make songs about virtually everything. For instance, 50 Cent favors a gangster style that reflects his tumultuous life in the ghetto, while Ludacris focuses on boasting in his high-energy club songs and Nas includes inspirational, thought-provoking themes in his rhymes.

Hip-Hop as a Lifestyle

Hip-hop's influence on popular culture has been immense. It is an integral part of the lives of millions of people in the United States and abroad. Classes on hip-hop culture and on the work of such rappers as 2Pac (later known as Tupac Shakur) and Lil' Kim are taught in a number of major American universities. Rap artists join their rock-and-roll contemporaries on tour and in performances at major sporting events such as the Super Bowl and the NBA All-Star Game. Hip-hop songs are among the most popular ringtones for cell phones, and hip-hop artists contribute to the soundtracks for video games and movies.

But hip-hop has also endured its share of doubters and controversy. In its formative years, hip-hop culture, along with its various manifestations, was dismissed as a fad. Embraced by the young generation, it created a rift with parents who thought that rapping was not music, that graffiti was not art, and that break dancing was not dancing. Furthermore, as rap became popular, its at times negative influence was bemoaned by a number of activists. Feminist groups have denounced the misogynistic lyrics of some rappers, religious figures have criticized the violent, "thuggish" work of gangsta rap artists, and civil rights organizations have boycotted several rappers because of their homophobic lyrics.

Despite these detractors, hip-hop has provided a sense of hope and purpose for millions of people. Hip-hop is considered by its practitioners and followers as the voice of the voiceless, the voice of youth, and a major cultural force. Hip-hop has given a generation of people hope that they could become successful and respected in any number of ways, whether by winning a DJ tournament, designing acclaimed artwork, choreographing the dance moves for a music video, starting their own business, or becoming a platinum rapper.

Indeed, Jay-Z, Lil Wayne, and Eminem are part of the select group of artists who are no longer looked at as just rappers. They are now personalities, entertainers who are among the most respected and powerful celebrities in the world. They all had a desire to make it as rappers, to be successful in their lives, and to achieve the American dream— and they all did it with the musical and cultural force known as hip-hop.

CHAPTER 1

The Roots of Hip-Hop Culture

Hip-hop culture was born in the mid-1970s in the Bronx, an impoverished section of New York City inhabited by a large segment of lower-class African Americans and Latinos. The increasingly poor borough was disintegrating because of crime, arson, housing abandonment, and overall neglect by its residents and their landlords. Many vacant, crumbling high-rise apartment buildings provided an ideal haven for illegal activities, including drug dealing, robbery, and murder.

Amid this chaos, a group of young black and Latino Bronx residents with few economic resources and a need to express themselves created their own entertainment with the materials available to them. They played the record collections of their parents to entertain themselves, they used the cardboard boxes littering the streets as dancing surfaces, and they used cans of spray paint to make their own art. The result was the birth of a new culture: hip-hop.

Hip-hop culture includes rapping, DJing, graffiti art, and B-boying, also known as break dancing. Rappers recite words over music, DJs play records and perform in front of an audience, and break-dancers perform an energetic style of dance that often includes exaggerated body movements and acrobatic moves, such as whirls. One of the earliest ways that hip-hop culture found expression, however, was through graffiti.

Graffiti Style

Though illegal, graffiti became popular in Philadelphia, Pennsylvania, in the 1960s as a way for people to express themselves in public places. By the 1970s it had spread to New York City. Some graffiti artists, also known as writers, were members of street gangs who wrote their gang names on walls and benches to mark their territory. Other graffiti artists who were not in gangs promoted themselves as artists by creating their own nicknames, or tags, to accompany their drawings. A few paid homage to their neighborhood by including in their tag the number of the street on which they lived. For example, some of the early graffiti artists were Taki 183, Joe 136, Julio 204, and Frank 207.

These graffiti artists often used bright colors to enhance their designs. They wrote their tags in a number of different styles, from basic print or cursive writing to more elaborate forms that included calligraphy-like designs and shading. Regardless of the design, the point of graffiti was for it to be seen, so the artists made sure that the color of the paint

Graffiti tags were particularly prevalent in subways and other trains in New York City in the 1970s. This piece by artist Henry Chalfant is entitled "We Drenched the City with Our Names."

they used was visible against the wall or backdrop on which they painted.

Graffiti writers made their biggest mark on the subway trains that traveled throughout the New York metropolitan area. While trains were parked in the train yard at night, graffiti writers went to work painting their exteriors. To the artists, subway cars were large, mobile canvases.

Although graffiti was seen as art by the people doing it, others did not share this view. People living in the wealthier sections of New York City looked at graffiti as a symbol of the decay of their city. People living in graffiti-filled areas bemoaned the art, which defaced buildings and reduced the attractiveness and value of property in their neighborhoods. They also resented the gang members who used graffiti to mark their territory. However, in the desolate Bronx environment, many young people turned to graffiti as a source of entertainment. They used it not only as a means of self-expression, but also, since it was illegal, as a way to rebel against the government that they felt ignored their desperate plight.

Kool DJ Herc Creates a Culture

Most of the graffiti artists had similar musical tastes. By listening to music, they and other young residents of the Bronx could temporarily escape their abysmal surroundings. These residents listened to soul artists such as Al Green and Marvin Gaye, funk practitioners James Brown and George Clinton, disco acts such as the Bee Gees and Chic, and the electronic group Kraftwerk, among many others.

One of these young music fans was Clive Campbell, better known by his stage name, Kool DJ Herc. He was born in Kingston, on the Caribbean island of Jamaica, and grew up listening to ska and reggae music, two energetic musical forms that originated in his homeland. An avid music fan and record collector, Herc (short for Hercules, the Greek warrior hero) was impressed by the sound systems used by disc jockeys in Jamaica. DJs are people who play and comment on recorded music, either on the radio, in dance clubs, or at concerts. The DJs that Herc watched as a child transported monstrous speakers and record collections to outdoor concerts given in front of hundreds, and sometimes thousands, of people.

In 1967, when he was twelve, Herc immigrated with his family to the Bronx, bringing his love for music with him. As he grew up, Herc decided he wanted to become a DJ. After collecting enough records and stereo equipment, he began hosting open-invitation block parties where he played music to entertain the people. To play the music loud enough, he created a sound system that he modeled after the mobile setups he had heard and seen in Jamaica.

With the help of his friends, Herc carted his enormous speakers, which often stood up to 6 feet (1.8m) tall, along with prized selections from his mammoth collection of more than one thousand records to the courtyards of public housing buildings and plugged his equipment into the lampposts. This pilfered electricity powered his turntables and allowed him to play music for the neighborhood for hours. Within months, the parties that Herc hosted drew an increasingly large and diverse group.

Many of the people gravitated to the parties, which were held on a smaller scale in the recreational rooms of apartment buildings, because the events were like going to a nightclub, but the attendees did not have to dress up or pay for admission. The parties were also easy to get to. Some participants could simply walk outside to the courtyard of their apartment building. For others, the parties were only a subway ride away. The events were an easy and convenient gathering point for a group of people with little disposable income and few inexpensive entertainment opportunities, especially for those who enjoyed dancing.

The Breaks

Herc noticed that people who enjoyed dancing at his DJ sessions became especially animated during certain kinds of songs, particularly funk songs when the music would "break" down, having the percussion instruments playing alone. People enjoyed dancing to the breaks more than any other portion of the song. Dancers also used the breaks to showcase specialized dance routines with complicated spinning and leg maneuvers.

With his DJ sessions becoming increasingly popular, Herc made a breakthrough in how a DJ works. He extended the breaks, making them the focal point of his DJ sets. To do this, he put a copy of the same song on each of his two turntables. A device known as a mixer, which DJs normally put between the two turntables to manipulate a record on one turntable without having to reach over the other turntable while it was playing, allowed Herc to switch between the two records. He would find the break on one record, play it, and then switch over to the same break section on the record on the second turntable, using a knob called a fader. Once he had practiced finding the breaks in songs, Herc could repeat them over and over again by using the mixer and fader to shift back and forth between the two copies of the same record.

The dancers at Herc's session loved his breaks. During these extended portions of the rhythm sections of songs, they were able to practice and experiment with moves that before had been limited to brief flashes during the climax of a song. Intricate footwork, spinning moves, and mechanical motion were the signature moves of the dancers. For example, they did headspins by standing on their heads and spinning around with their arms outstretched and legs raised toward the sky. Another was the moonwalk, in which the dancers slide backward as their feet and legs appear to be moving forward.

Herc called these dancers break boys, since they danced to the breaks. The dancers became known as B-boys for short. The early B-boy crews included the Shaka Zulu Kings and the Shaka Zulu Queens. They traveled the Bronx and other parts of New York, going from party to party to showcase their dancing.

Afrika Bambaataa: Master of Records

The parties that Herc hosted included other DJs besides himself. Among them were Grandmaster Caz (later of the Cold Crush Brothers), Grandmaster Flash, and a young

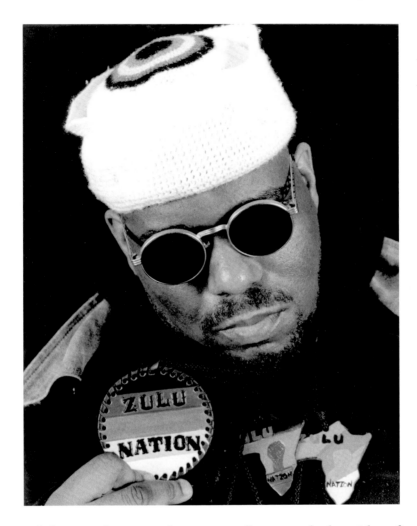

Afrika Bambaataa formed the peaceful organization Zulu Nation in the 1970s to popularize and promote the developing hip-hop culture in New York.

Afrika Bambaataa, who eventually earned the title of Master of Records because of his immense knowledge of a wide range of musical styles, including rock, soul, funk, R&B, and reggae. Besides being a DJ, Bambaataa was also a member of a Bronx street gang called the Black Spades. Eventually, however, Bambaataa came to believe that gang warfare was destroying his beloved city. Gangs sold drugs and killed people, and Bambaataa believed they had to be stopped. Bambaataa later reflected on the impact gangs were having in New York during the 1970s: "I saw it was time to move the gangs in a different direction, before we all wound up dead or in jail."[1] To do so, Bambaataa formed the Zulu Nation, a peaceful organization that aimed to popularize and promote the developing hip-hop culture. It adopted the motto "Peace, unity, love, happiness, and fun."[2]

Using a pair of turntables his mother had bought him for his high school graduation, Bambaataa quickly established himself as one of the premier DJs of the burgeoning hip-hop culture, with a reputation to rival that of Kool DJ Herc. He used a wide range of records from any musical style he could collect, from the fiery, funky rock music of James Brown to the computerized sounds of Kraftwerk. Bambaataa later became known as the Godfather of Hip-Hop.

Battles Begin as Hip-Hop Parties Grow

With Herc and Bambaataa becoming celebrities in their neighborhoods, competition between DJs began to develop. DJs began unofficial rivalries with each other to see

Party Flyers Spread the Word

More than a decade before the advent of the Internet and long before hip-hop events were promoted on television and radio, flyers were the main way to announce hip-hop events to fans. The flyers were handed out in the streets and at other parties or events and provided details such as the address of the club, the evening's host, the time of the party, the performers, and the date.

Famous graffiti artists designed many of the flyers. Initially, the flyers featured the artists' logos and silhouettes of the acts. Eventually, photos of the artists, such as the Funky Four, Fantastic Romantic Freaks, Jazzy Jay, Kurtis Blow, and Whodini, were included.

At the end of the 1980s, flyers were sometimes replaced in favor of posters, which were often just larger versions of flyers. These posters were routinely attached to telephone poles, trees, and other objects. Today, flyers preserved by hip-hop fans from the late 1970s and early 1980s are sometimes displayed in museums.

whose sound system was the loudest and whose sets were best received by the crowd. Bambaataa later recalled his early DJ sets:

I would come with 16, 20 crates of vinyl, and play from 9 till 4 in the morning, switching records every minute or two. We were always trying to outdo each other, play records more obscure than any other deejay, scratching out the titles so other deejays couldn't copy us. People would tell me they didn't like salsa music, but I'd slam some on 'em with a break beat, and they'd be dancing to it. I'd work in calypso and rock, the Monkees, Kraftwerk, James Brown, and just for kicks an old Coke commercial or "My Boyfriend's Back." You came to my shows, you were going on a musical journey.[3]

The high-energy music played by renowned DJs such as Kool DJ Herc and Afrika Bambaataa transformed sets into more than just an opportunity to listen to a smorgasbord of sounds. At these parties people could watch B-boy crews such as the Rock Steady Crew, the most respected B-boy group because it was known to have the best dancers. Besides watching the B-boys perform seemingly gravity-defying dance moves, attendees could associate with the

A member of the Rock Steady Crew, the most respected B-boy group in the early years of hip-hop, performs at the Roxy nightclub in 1984.

graffiti artists who were literally making their mark on subway trains and buildings throughout the city or just soak in the atmosphere of the hip-hop scene.

The people attending these gatherings did their own unofficial recruiting by urging their friends, neighbors, and family members to join them at the hip-hop parties. Yet the scene remained largely unknown to the rest of the world.

The Itch to Scratch

DJs remained the stars of hip-hop gatherings, so up-and-coming DJs were eager to find ways to separate themselves from other DJs. In 1975 Grand Wizard Theodore, a high school student and aspiring DJ, developed another asset to help DJs impress audiences. But unlike Kool DJ Herc, who deliberately incorporated elongated breaks into his DJ routine, Theodore created his addition to hip-hop culture by accident and in isolation. His invention: scratching. Scratching occurs when the DJ moves a record back and forth against the needle, creating a scratching sound. In a 2001 interview Grand Wizard Theodore recalled how he invented scratching:

> I used to come home from school and go in my room and practice a lot and this particular day I came home and played my music too loud and my mom was banging on the door and when she opened the door I turned the music down but the music was still playing in my headphones and she was screaming "If you don't turn the music down you better turn it off" and I had turned down the speakers but I was still holding the record and moving it back and forth listening in my headphones and I thought "This really sounded [like] something [special] . . . interjecting another record with another record." And as time went by I experimented with it trying other records and soon it became scratching.[4]

Grand Wizard Theodore also created the needle drop, an important but often overlooked DJ tactic. The needle drop occurs when a DJ drops the needle on a record at exactly the point he wants the record to play without having to cue

Boom Boxes Blast Rap Music

Around 1980, personal stereos became a popular way for people in New York to listen to music while they were outside. These personal stereos, known as boom boxes because the music would "boom" from the speakers, could easily be carried from one location to the next. They typically got both AM and FM radio stations and had either one or two cassette decks. Cassette tapes from early hip-hop events were often played on these personal stereos.

In 1980 only a few rap songs had been released commercially on record and there were no radio shows dedicated to playing rap music. This made the boom box essential for rap music to be heard throughout New York City. Indeed, the mobility of the boom box allowed rap to spread quickly throughout the streets of New York, as a person could carry it along on the subway, into a store while shopping, or onto a basketball court while watching a game. Radio owners personalized their stereos by adding a strap so they could sling it over their shoulder or by "tagging" the radio with graffiti.

it up or listen to it. Theodore did this by looking at the record itself. Records were made out of vinyl. On each side is one long, continuous groove that circles the record dozens of times. When certain musical changes, such as a guitar solo, take place in a song, the spacing between the coils of the groove changes, becoming either wider or narrower. After listening to a song several times, a DJ can look at the vinyl, tell by the spacing where such musical changes occur, and thus know where to drop the needle to play a desired section.

As more and more DJs entered the hip-hop field, they continued to develop, refine, and enhance their routines. The use of breaks, scratching, and needle drops, among other techniques, enlivened the DJs' sets. The DJ had evolved from someone who simply played records and worked a crowd to someone who knew how to keep party-goers dancing from the start of the party until the last song was played. As the one in control of the party, the DJ was the center of hip-hop culture, which got its name because of the way the dancers would "hip" and "hop" (jump and move) to the music.

Rappers Emerge

To keep the crowds entertained during breaks in their sets, the DJs hooked up microphones to their sound systems and spoke to the audience. They said simple phrases such as "And ya don't stop" and "To the beat, y'all." But during the sets themselves, the DJs, who had to focus on keeping the party going by playing the right records, had their friends keep the crowd engaged by talking on the microphone. Such a vocalist was called an MC, short for master of ceremonies.

At first, the main purpose of the MC was to praise the DJ. For instance, an MC might say that Grandmaster Flash "cuts faster" than the competition, meaning that he could cut, or scratch, more effectively and efficiently than other DJs. "Grandmaster cuts faster" also sounded clever because it rhymed. The MC in this instance was thus rhyming and praising Grandmaster Flash simultaneously.

The MCs soon became popular attractions and started talking more and more frequently during the parties. They often spoke in rhyme and engaged in call-and-response with their audience. For example, the MC would say to the crowd, "Everybody say, 'Ho!'" and those in attendance would respond by yelling "Ho!" This call-and-response created a lively atmosphere, similar to that found in some churches, and made the audience feel as though they were part of the entertainment, not just being entertained. Besides "Everybody say, 'Ho!'" the MCs popularized famous sayings such as "What's your Zodiac sign?" and "Throw your hands in the air like you just don't care."

By the late 1970s the MCs were becoming stars in their own right and were drawing their own crowds. DJs and club and party promoters began pitting aspiring MCs against each other in sharp exchanges of wit called battles.

Spoken-Word Poets Precede Rappers

At least five years before rappers began emerging in the Bronx section of New York, a number of politically minded spoken-word poets were reciting their poetry over music. The Last Poets, Gil Scott-Heron, and the Watts Prophets were among this group of performers, who are often considered the first generation of rappers. Each of these three acts infused their poetry with political commentary. Their work included condemnation of white oppression, affronts to then-President Ronald Reagan, and championing of the black power movement.

On the other side of the artistic spectrum was a host of rhyming spoken-word artists who favored comedic material. Rudy Ray Moore, known by the self-proclaimed titles "Godfather of Rap" and "The World's First and Only Rappin' Comedian," is best known for his work as the character Dolemite. In 1970 Moore released *Eat Out More Often*, his first comedy record. Its tales regale listeners with frank discussions of sex. As his comedic career took off, Moore's wild characters and their remarkable adventures and accomplishments earned him a rabid fan base. Blowfly was among those who released albums similar to Moore's in the early 1970s.

Now, instead of making the DJ the focus of the action by rapping about the joys of partying and the merits of their DJ, the MCs vied for the spotlight against each other. Like the DJs before them, MCs took great pride in being able to entertain crowds and deliver the most memorable rhymes, which often included boasts about their rhyming abilities.

During the MC battles, the art of freestyle rhyming evolved. This kind of rapping is defined by MCs who make up rhymes on the spot. Typically, these clever performers describe the room in which they are rhyming, the crowd they are performing for, or the clothing or look of their opponent, which they often criticize.

Hip-Hop Spreads

MCs could use the bragging rights from a battle to land hosting gigs at area clubs and even headline their own shows.

Club managers started hiring DJs and MCs, now also called rappers because of the way they would rap (slang for "converse" or "talk") with their audience, because it was clear that they could draw crowds. Some of the early clubs that showcased rap were Harlem World, Disco Fever, and the Rock Steady Lounge. The success of these shows convinced the shrewd entrepreneurs among the DJs, rappers, and club owners that they could sell recordings of the events. Soon, cassette tapes featuring the work of the emerging DJs and rappers in New York City spread across the country.

Disco Fever in the Bronx was one of the first clubs to showcase rap music.

These recordings allowed listeners to visit a world that had previously been available only by attending a party or a hip-hop night at a club in New York City. Almost as soon as they were made, copies of the cassette tapes were sent, borrowed, and shared with friends and relatives. In this way, DJs, rappers, and fans created hip-hop followers across the country. People were drawn to the new style of music that was typified by breaks and the rappers speaking in rhymes over the music to an energetic audience. Hip-hop was set to graduate from an underground phenomenon into a movement embraced by music executives eager to profit from it.

CHAPTER 2

Hip-Hop Gains Momentum

As hip-hop culture gained momentum in the New York underground scene, DJs such as Grandmaster Flash and DJ Hollywood, and rappers such as Busy Bee and Melle Mel, drew hundreds of people to nightclubs. Block parties hosted by Kool DJ Herc, Afrika Bambaataa, and others remained popular gathering places for B-boys, graffiti artists, and aspiring DJs and rappers. Propelled by a host of creative and energetic artists, the fledgling hip-hop culture was one event away from emerging on a national scale. That event was a song.

"Rapper's Delight"

Rap and hip-hop took a major step forward in 1979 with the release of "Rapper's Delight" by the Sugarhill Gang. It was only the second rap song ever recorded and released commercially. [The first was "King Tim III (Personality Jock)" by the Fatback Band.] Sugar Hill Records owner Sylvia Robinson, who had been a successful R&B singer and songwriter before becoming a record company executive, wanted to record a novelty record she hoped would cash in on the hip-hop trend. She assembled three little-known rappers, Wonder Mike, Master Gee, and Big Bank Hank, and had them record a song. The result, "Rapper's Delight," which borrows its groove from "Good Times" by the disco group Chic, became a smash hit.

Each rapper contributed simple, playful lyrics that welcome everyone to the hip-hop world. Early in his first verse, Wonder Mike invites people of all races and nationalities to join the group's musical party. The Sugarhill Gang fills the rest of the song with other themes that many people could relate to: an affinity for flashy fashion, the desire to attract members of the opposite sex, and the awkwardness of having an uncomfortable experience with a friend.

Several future music superstars were among the more than 2 million people who bought a copy of the single. In fact, "Rapper's Delight" was the first record that popular R&B singer Mary J. Blige, who emerged in the 1990s, ever bought. She explains, "It was the newest thing, so everyone was running to get it."[5]

Rap Makes Commercial Strides

"Rapper's Delight" eventually reached number thirty-six on the pop singles chart and peaked at number four on the

LL Cool J Finds a "Delight"-ful Inspiration

LL Cool J is one of rap music's most enduring figures. He released his first album in 1985 and is one of the few rappers from that era who is still popular today. Like many rappers who emerged in the 1980s, LL Cool J was a fan of the Sugarhill Gang and their hit single "Rapper's Delight." Below, LL Cool J explains the impact of the Sugarhill Gang on his life in his autobiography, I Make My Own Rules:

It was 1979 and the Sugar Hill Gang was blowing up the charts with "Rapper's Delight." They had taken Chic's "Good Times," a song that had been out for a while, but was still rocking, and turned it into a rap song. It changed the face of music and it was the Sugar Hill Gang, along with Afrika Bambaataa and the Zulu Nation, who got me into rap. A lot of people look back at Sugar Hill as some corny group, but to me they brought rap to a whole other level. They put rap on the map.

I was 11 when I first saw the Sugar Hill Gang perform. It was at the old Harlem Armory, not too far from the Apollo. They had been promoting this concert for more than a month in my neighborhood. There were flyers on every tree, light post, and brick wall in St. Albans and I wanted to be there. Because for the first time, there was a form of music that literally spoke to me. Sugar Hill had my voice. They rapped about things I could relate to or wanted to relate to. They rapped about women and money, and about money and women. They had checkbooks, credit cards, cars, and clothes.

LL Cool J with Karen Hunter. *I Make My Own Rules.* New York: St. Martin's Press, 1997, p. 63.

R&B chart. The popular song was for many people their introduction to rap. After all, anyone who did not live in or visit the New York metropolitan area could not experience hip-hop culture firsthand.

The success of "Rapper's Delight" convinced a few record company executives that this new form of music could be profitable. The song demonstrated that this new art form could be mass-produced, bought, sold, and enjoyed on a national scale. Less than a year later Kurtis Blow became the first rapper to get a recording contract with a major record company, when he signed with Mercury Records in 1980. It was a major accomplishment for the genre, which at that time was still a virtually unknown commodity. Another breakthrough came in 1981, when the Funky 4+1, a rap group best known for its festive single "That's the Joint," was featured on the hit comedy sketch program *Saturday Night Live*, thereby becoming the first rap group to make a national television appearance.

Most major corporations and media entities, however, ignored rap. They looked at the new form of music as a fad, like disco, that would soon disappear. This lack of interest from corporate America forced rap, much like rock and roll before it, to develop without the influence of major record companies.

"The Message" Strikes a Chord

Sugar Hill Records used the success of "Rapper's Delight" to become a prominent rap label. The Sugarhill Gang followed up the song with the 1980 cut "8th Wonder," which peaked at number fifteen on the R&B charts, and the 1981 single "Apache," which peaked at number thirteen on the R&B charts. But the next landmark release from Sugar Hill Records came from Grandmaster Flash & the Furious Five, a respected rap collective anchored by renowned DJ Grandmaster Flash and rapper Melle Mel. The group released "The Message" on the label in 1982. It became one of the most influential and significant rap singles of all time.

Unlike the few commercially released rap songs that preceded it, "The Message" describes the desolate neighborhoods that many members of the hip-hop culture called home. It is a dark, somber song that stands in stark contrast to the party music, brimming with braggadocio, that most rappers were releasing at the time.

A number of prominent rappers, from gangsta rap pioneer Schoolly D to respected lyricist Common, cite "The Message" as their reason to rhyme. Gangsta rapper Jayo Felony recalls the impact that "The Message" and Melle Mel made on his life:

"The Message," that's when I finally really got into

writing raps, when I heard that song. Before then, I never really used to hear people cuss on records and at the end of the record, I heard him say, "Get in the goddamn car," and that was like the first time I heard somebody say anything like that and the raps he was talking about were real street. "Don't push me, 'cause I'm close to the edge/I'm trying not to lose my head." That song inspired me to rap.[6]

Rap Style Gets Tougher

In addition to the darker tone of "The Message," people were drawn to the song because the rhymes of Melle Mel were

Grandmaster Flash & the Furious Five's 1982 release "The Message" became one of the most influential rap singles of all time.

more sophisticated and complicated than those of other rappers such as the Sugarhill Gang or Kurtis Blow. The ascension of Melle Mel gave rap a street edge. Mel was a seasoned veteran of the mid-1970s rap circuit who won a number of rhyming battles because of his tremendous rhyming talent and his ability to construct complex rhymes. With a commanding voice, riveting rhymes, and an intimidating stage presence, Mel (also known as Grandmaster Melle Mel) was the type of rapper that other rappers aspired to be. He was articulate, clever, tough, and, most of all, respected by the hip-hop community.

By contrast, the Sugarhill Gang members—Master Gee, Wonder Mike, and Big Bank Hank—favored a simple pattern that often incorporated obvious rhymes, such as "cat" with "hat" or "feet" and "seat." Other rappers, such as Busy Bee and Kurtis Blow, favored a similarly simple, good-natured, laid-back rhyming approach that could not keep up with the lyrical advance of rappers such as Melle Mel, Kool Moe Dee of the Treacherous 3, or T La Rock, whose multisyllabic words and fast delivery patterns required great skill to perform without stumbling over the lyrics.

The Rap Sound

Even though "Rapper's Delight" is a party record and "The Message" reflects the harsh reality of living in an American ghetto, the two songs share a number of similarities. Like most of the rap music from this period, the use of instruments in these songs was minimal. Unlike songs in other genres of music, which included a variety of instruments (sometimes with intricate progressions), rap music of this era typically featured only drums, a bass line, and maybe a keyboard effect or two. Unless the songs were recorded with a house band, as was the case with some of the recordings produced by Sugar Hill Records, few other instruments were used.

Part of the reason rap artists used minimal instrumentation was that, as outsiders in the music business, they lacked access to state-of-the-art studios. Instead, they often recorded music in amateur home studios that did not have the capability to produce the type of comparatively complex, layered recording favored by established studios. Therefore, rappers not backed by a house band often did their rhyming over only a drum track that came from a drum machine, a piece of studio equipment that makes a variety of drum sounds that can sound remarkably similar to those produced by a live drummer.

Many musicians and record company executives said that rap, with its sparse sound and style, was not music because its songs do not contain melody, a rhythmically organized sequence of single tones so related to one another as to make up a particular musical passage or idea. In fact, many R&B and funk artists went out of their way in interviews to discredit rap music.

But the criticism did not stop rap from evolving. Afrika Bambaataa's 1981 single with the Jazzy Five, "Jazzy Sensation," set the stage for his landmark work with Soul Sonic Force (also written as Soulsonic Force). Their 1982 single "Planet Rock," which borrows the melody from Kraftwerk's quirky "Trans-Europe Express," helped pioneer a new sound that relied on keyboards and electronic sound effects to accent the music. Many of these sounds recalled a computer blip or the chirping of birds. Bambaataa and his group rapped and sang much in the way that old funk bands did: intermittently, with computer-altered voices and with long breaks in which the music played uninterrupted. Bambaataa later recalled how he invented his new sound, which he dubbed "electro-funk":

> I learned from James [Brown], Sly [Stone] and Uncle George [Clinton]. But I was also listening to Yellow Magic Orchestra, Kraftwerk and Gary Numan, and getting off on the electronic music in John Carpenter's *Halloween* movies and *Assault on Precinct 13*. I wanted to be the first black group to come out with that sound. So I formed Soulsonic Force and invented electro-funk.[7]

Hip-Hop Hits the Big Screen

As rap continued evolving with new sounds and styles, graffiti, B-boying, and DJing were also making major contributions to hip-hop culture. The festive video for "Rapper's

Graffiti as "Opera"

In the book Hip Hop Files: Photographs, 1979–1984, Style Wars *director Tony Silver recalls how he was introduced to the graffiti lifestyle that he depicted in his landmark film:*

> My original idea for what became *Style Wars* was a short film about a b-boy crew. . . . Henry [Chalfant, *Style Wars*' co-director] and I talked and I saw his photos, which were amazing, and I got more and more excited about a larger film that would have a number of elements and music. The problem was the subject seemed so big; it was hard to envision the shape of it. One night, Henry and I and Kathy, his wife, were talking about the movie. Kathy, who is an actress, went into this riff, this aria, "You have to understand how dramatic this is. You are going to a scary train yard in the middle of the night, you have a bag of cans, you're hanging off the side of a train painting a mural in just one night that will cover the whole side of a subway car. And any minute you'll be chased by the cops." To me, it sounded like an opera. You risk everything to go to the edge, a struggle for recognition against all odds, not some made-up story—but an opera that's real.

Quoted in Martha Cooper. *Hip Hop Files: Photographs, 1979–1984.* Berlin, Germany: From Here to Fame, 2004, p. 168.

Delight" features B-boys showcasing some of their dance moves, while the gritty video for "The Message" takes place on a rundown city street with buildings covered with graffiti.

The 1982 film *Wild Style* shows how interwoven and interrelated each component of hip-hop was at that point. The movie has several story lines, among them the struggle that a graffiti writer goes through to balance his personal life with his love for his art. The movie features graffiti writers, rappers, DJs, and B-boys in prominent roles, giving attention to each segment of the flourishing hip-hop culture.

Wild Style, the first authentic and earnest look at the culture, is considered the definitive hip-hop movie.

Much as cassette tapes and "Rapper's Delight" had done a few years earlier, *Wild Style* gave many people their first exposure to hip-hop. But *Wild Style* was especially significant because it provided a visual look at the culture. Now, people could emulate the graffiti artists, rappers, and B-boys they saw on screen, allowing hip-hop to grow quickly in the underground and also leading to the 1983 graffiti film *Style Wars*.

In 2007 Grand Wizard Theodore performs at the twenty-fifth anniversary celebration for Wild Style, *which is widely considered the definitive movie about hip-hop.*

B-boying Takes Center Stage

While rap was looked at with skepticism by the mainstream business world, B-boying was the first element of hip-hop culture to be embraced by corporate America. Released in 1983, the smash film *Flashdance*, starring Jennifer Beals as an aspiring ballet dancer, also features Crazy Legs, Mr. Freeze, and Prince Ken Swift, members of the seminal B-boy group Rock Steady Crew.

The next year, *Breakin'* hit movie theaters. The film centers on a jazz dancer and two B-boys who team up and become popular street dancers. Television commercials, endorsements, and other deals soon followed for B-boys who had garnered media attention from their film and in-person performances. Today, hip-hop documentary film producer and one-time professional B-boy QD3 recalls the impact of B-boys: "B-boying was the first thing that drew attention to hip-hop, period. It was really the spark that made it go mainstream. Before that it was contained. *Flashdance* came out and break dancing was the bridge that we crossed to go into the rest of the world to some degree. [Break-dancers] were the first superstars."[8]

Rap Gets Media Exposure

As B-boying and graffiti were enjoying commercial exposure, rap was making strides of its own. By October 1983 both Mr. Magic and Kool DJ Red Alert, prominent DJs in the hip-hop community, had radio shows on the New York airwaves. These shows, the first commercial radio outlets to showcase rap music, were critical in spreading the genre throughout New York and the rest of the country. A person who had never heard a rap song could now turn on the radio and hear entire programs dedicated to rap. In fact, many of Mr. Magic's and Kool DJ Red Alert's radio shows were recorded and shared among rap fans, much like the recordings of early rap performances.

Also in 1983 came the debut of *Video Music Box*. Entrepreneur Ralph McDaniels of Brooklyn, a section of New York City, hosted the video music show, which aired on public television and at the time was the only program showing hip-hop videos. The first video the program aired was *5 Minutes of Funk* by rap trio Whodini.

The breakthrough of rap on radio and video provided the perfect platform for Kurtis Blow. On his 1984 hit "Basketball," the good-natured rapper cleverly weaves the names of basketball stars such as Dr. J and Moses Malone into his rap about his love for the sport. The video for the song, which features Blow rapping on a basketball court, was one of the early examples of a rap song that garnered considerable attention from those not in the hip-hop audience.

With all elements of hip-hop culture making their mark in society, rappers started touring, particularly in Europe, where the culture was openly embraced. In 1982 Afrika Bambaataa organized the first European hip-hop tour. He later recalled his world vision for hip-hop: "I was taking music from all over the planet to spread this new sound all over the planet. I wanted to break it in the Tri-State area, then across the U.S.A. and then the world. I had a vision that this was more than just party music for the ghetto."[9]

DJs and Rappers Emerge from Hip-Hop

As DJs, rap songs, and rap artists began to enjoy more and more success in the mid-1980s, graffiti and B-boying

Gold Chains Become Prized Possessions

In the mid-1980s gold-plated chains became one of hip-hop's most prominent fashion statements. Nicknamed "rope chains" because many of them were thicker than rope, these gold chains were worn by nearly every rapper of the era.

The chains served several purposes. In addition to being a fashion statement, the chains were a status symbol that signified that the rapper was accomplished, as the chains were expensive and most people living in the New York ghettos where the rappers were raised could not afford them.

Many rappers of this era wore one rope chain. But in the next few years, several rap acts, including Eric. B & Rakim and Big Daddy Kane, took the trend a step further by wearing several chains at once. No rapper, though, made gold chains as prominent as Slick Rick, the playful storytelling rapper who wore so many chains that people wondered how he did not tip over from the weight.

As gold became common, it fell out of favor in the mid-1990s, and rappers looked for another jewelry fashion statement. They found one in platinum chains, which took the place of the gold rope chains.

became little more than gimmicks to corporate America. Graffiti was still illegal, and even though some graffiti artists were commissioned, they had to paint in a controlled, often indoor environment that removed the thrill of the forbidden, as well as the rebellious edge of the art.

As the art world started looking elsewhere for cutting-edge work, B-boys also started losing some of their popularity. Instructional break-dancing tapes were sold on television, making it seem as though anyone who bought the tapes and a dancing mat could be an instant B-boy star. As with other skills, it took years of practice for B-boys to perfect their moves. But companies eager to cash in on the break-dancing trend portrayed these extraordinary dance skills as easy to acquire.

Although break dancing became common in mainstream culture, rap was still an art form on the fringes. Major labels had yet to fully embrace the new music, allowing independent record companies such as Sugar Hill, Jive, Reality, Profile, and Tommy Boy to corner the rap market. These small companies, free to pursue any artists they deemed worthy without having to worry about approval

The members of Run-D.M.C. and their posse pose in their Queens neighborhood, Hollis, in 1984.

from a corporation, signed a variety of rap talent that reflected the diverse range of people who made up the hip-hop community.

The rap trio Whodini, for example, wrote creative, narrative raps about social outcasts and love that were performed over keyboard-driven music, while Doug E. Fresh showcased his beat-boxing skills on a number of his early recordings. Beat boxing is the art of using the mouth to create percussion sounds that serve as a beat for someone else to rap to. Beat boxing enjoyed exposure in several 1980s movies, including the comedies *Police Academy* and *Disorderlies*, which starred the rap group Fat Boys.

But the breakout group of this era was Run-D.M.C. This trio from Queens, a borough of New York City, featured rappers Run and D.M.C., and DJ Jam Master Jay. The first release from the group was the seminal 1983 single "It's Like That/Sucker MC's." The group presented itself as common guys on the street who had much in common with their fans. Run, who later became an ordained minister and changed his name to Reverend Run, recalls, "One big part of Run-D.M.C.'s success was our catchy rhymes that made you think or sometimes laugh. No violence or harsh language, just thinking, laughing, and having fun."[10]

Other Musicians Embrace Hip-Hop

As Run-D.M.C. helped expand rap's commercial base in the early 1980s, musicians who appreciated the grassroots nature of rap also embraced the emerging music, giving it some credibility in the musical community. Deborah Harry raps on "Rapture," a 1981 single from her rock group, Blondie, in which she mentions hip-hop celebrity Fab Five Freddy (also written as Fab 5 Freddie) and uses the hip-hop slang word *fly*, another way to say that someone or something is cool. Jazz musician Herbie Hancock teams with Grand-mixer D.ST (who later changed his name to Grandmixer DXT) for the 1983 hit "Rockit." The video for that song features D.ST scratching and was the first time most people saw a DJ performing a scratch. R&B singer Chaka Khan features Melle Mel on her 1984 single "I Feel for You," marking the first time that an established R&B singer collaborated with a rapper on a single.

Each of these singles gave different audiences an opportunity to experience hip-hop culture when paired with a type of music they already enjoyed. Music fans no longer had to seek out rap. It was popping up in a variety of other music styles. With rock, jazz, and R&B musicians embracing it, rap and, by default, hip-hop culture were slowly increasing in visibility and influence. As it continued developing and enjoying more and more success, rap music started earning coverage in mainstream publications such as rock magazine *Spin* and the *Village Voice*, a respected New York–based weekly newspaper. With its artists pushing themselves creatively and more and more independent record companies releasing rap songs, the genre was ready for its next big step.

CHAPTER 3

The Golden Era of Rap

By 1984 rappers including Run-D.M.C., Kurtis Blow, Whodini, and Fat Boys were popular enough to mount the landmark Fresh Fest Tour, the first national rap tour. These lyrically advanced acts had replaced the call-and-response and rhymers of the 1970s. Other than Run-D.M.C., however, this set of acts was itself about to be replaced during the golden era of rap, the years from approximately 1986 to 1989.

During this period, rap enjoyed an explosion in the range, skill, and talent of rappers. Rappers focused on a variety of lyrical topics and presented themselves in a variety of guises, representing virtually every segment of society: hippies, gangsters, party people, political activists, lovers, materialists, poets, and lyrical enthusiasts. Indeed, rappers of this era went well beyond the elementary party rhymes that the first and second generations of rappers had often employed, crafting ingenious raps about everything from dating to government corruption.

Rap Replaces Hip-Hop Culture

As rap enjoyed a creative explosion during the golden era, the other three components of hip-hop culture began to fade from the spotlight, especially B-boying and graffiti.

Although both survived, they were marginalized by rappers and, to a lesser extent, DJs.

The DJ was still a prominent part of live performances, providing input on the music. But for the first time, the other elements of hip-hop were used merely to supplement the rapper. For example, there might be a set of B-boys dancing in a rap video, but they were no longer the focal point. Rappers and the music they were producing were now taking center stage.

Sampling Becomes Prominent

In the early years of rap, artists such as the Sugarhill Gang, Grandmaster Flash & the Furious Five, and Kurtis Blow often rapped over live instrumentation that borrowed guitar rhythms, bass lines, and drum patterns from other songs, including, most famously, the Sugarhill Gang's usage of Chic's "Good Times" for "Rapper's Delight."

Following this habit of duplicating other artists' music, rap producers in the golden era of rap began "sampling" other songs, a practice that would permanently alter the direction of rap. Sampling occurs when a portion of a song from another recording is copied onto a piece of studio equipment called a sampler, which allows the original piece of music to be used on a new record. It is literally a sample, or portion or segment, of the original song. By using this technique, the rappers and their producers no longer needed to have musicians actually play music in order to make a song.

Samples typically last from four to eight measures, but they can also be shorter or longer, depending on the wishes of the artist or producer. The samples are often matched with a drum pattern, also potentially sampled, that fits the same tempo. In addition to samples of music, samples of singers, speeches, sound effects, and other noises and sounds are used. For instance, the screeching of soul singer James Brown was a favorite sample of early rap producers.

Run-D.M.C. Walks to Superstardom

Run-D.M.C. was one of the major beneficiaries of the idea of sampling. The group's third album, 1986's *Raising Hell*, became a multiplatinum success thanks in large part to the song "Walk This Way," a collaboration with the rock group Aerosmith. Run-D.M.C. originally planned on sampling the guitar riff Aerosmith had used on its song of the same

Run-D.M.C. Dresses Hip-Hop

In his spiritual memoir, It's Like That, *rapper Reverend Run explains the significance of the fashion his group Run-D.M.C. introduced:*

How we dressed was just as innovative as our sound. Run-D.M.C. pioneered a whole new way of dressing. We would have on sweat suits and black hats and unlaced Adidas. It was funny how we got that look. [Group member Jam Master] Jay was responsible for our dress code.

It was around 1984 and we were making money, and Jay bought whatever he wanted. One day Jay wore this incredible outfit. He was walking down Jamaica Avenue, the main shopping drag in Queens, and he had on all this expensive stuff: leather pants and a leather jacket, Adidas, a big gold rope, a black hat, and some Gazelle glasses. Everybody was checking him out, because he had on everything that everybody else wanted. (Jay could afford everything because we were making fifteen hundred to two thousand dollars for every performance. And we were working hard for the money. We could do two

shows in Brooklyn and two shows in Queens and Yonkers all in the same night if we started around 7:00 p.m. and things were scheduled right.)

You might see somebody with a rope or some Adidas or some Gazelles but not every one of them on at the same time. Jay was walking down Jamaica Avenue and it was like everybody wanted to snatch something from him because he had it going on. I mean nobody had everything: the glasses, the leather, the shoes, and the gold rope.

So we were doing well and Jay just was helping to create a nationwide trend and didn't know it. [My brother] Russell later refined the look by matching everything up so the appearance was cool but neat. But it was Jay who first influenced our look.

When the albums blew up [became popular], so did our look. Almost every young person in America tried to emulate us in some way.

The Reverend Run with Curtis L. Taylor. *It's Like That.* New York: St. Martin's Press, 2000, p. 41.

name a decade earlier. But at the behest of producer Rick Rubin, Run-D.M.C. contacted Aerosmith and eventually performed with guitarist Joe Perry and singer Steven Tyler on "Walk This Way."

With "Walk This Way," rap and rock created common ground that garnered the interest of fans of each genre. The video for "Walk This Way" marked a watershed in rap's development, as it was played in heavy rotation on the music video channel MTV. For many people not already interested in rap, "Walk This Way" was the rap song that they enjoyed, and the video gave them their first taste of hip-hop fashion. Run-D.M.C. had been developing its look, which featured black hats, black jeans, black jackets, gold chains, and white Adidas sneakers without shoelaces, for years.

Another *Raising Hell* single was "My Adidas." Here, Run-D.M.C. pays homage to its favorite shoe and, in effect, identifies itself with the brand. Musician and producer Sean "Diddy" Combs, a Run-D.M.C. fan, recalls seeing the group perform when he was a kid. "I was at the Raising Hell Tour at Madison Square Garden [in 1986], and Run-DMC held up their Adidas and told everybody in the crowd to hold up their Adidas," he says. "I swear, 20,000 people held up their sneakers. I remember I was like, 'I wanna do that one day.'"[11]

LL Cool J Makes Rap Sexy

The music of Run-D.M.C. was mostly gritty, aggressive, and bombastic, typical of rap music at the time. Even though the group had a sizable female following, some women found rap too abrasive, loud, and unrefined. Many women felt as though no rapper was speaking to them.

LL Cool J filled that void by catering to women in some of his music and soon became rap's first sex symbol. His debut album, 1985's *Radio*, was better known for such rugged selections as "I Can't Live Without My Radio," "Rock the Bells," and "I Need a Beat" than its songs geared to women, "Dear Yvette" and "I Want You." With the release of "I Need Love" two years later, however, LL Cool J was established as a ladies' man. After all, his name stands for Ladies Love Cool James.

Some of LL Cool J's music was geared toward women, helping make him rap's first sex symbol.

LL Cool J endured criticism from the rap community for making hip-hop love songs. Many of his detractors felt that, by making love songs, LL Cool J was diluting rap, making the genre soft and taking away its edge. Nonetheless, his albums also contained several harder-edged hip-hop songs that appealed to rap fans of either gender eager to hear his clever braggadocio rhymes and aggressive beats. By taking a creative risk, LL Cool J expanded rap's lyrical scope and almost single-handedly brought rap a new wave of female fans.

Female Rappers Make Their Mark

During the golden era of rap, when LL Cool J was rising to stardom, the previously male-dominated rap genre experienced an explosion of female talent. Much as LL Cool J had done, these female rappers increased rap's fan base and expanded their reach by making music that was not as abrasive and confrontational as that of their male counterparts.

Rappers Respond in Song

In the 1970s rappers battled against one another in live settings. The crowds, eager to hear one rapper make fun of the other using improvised rhymes, cheered the most potent rhymes from the artists participating in these battles. In 1981 Kool Moe Dee defeated Busy Bee in the most famous live rap battle.

As rap began to be recorded, the battles took on a new form: the response record. Many artists launched their careers by responding to the songs of other rappers, even though most of the time these responses were not justified—or even provoked. After all, for many of the respondents, this was their first release. Responding to a song, though, ensured them an audience.

An early example of this trend include Roxanne Shante's "Roxanne's Revenge," which was recorded after U.T.F.O.'s 1984 hit "Roxanne Roxanne," in which each of the three rappers in the group explained their different reasons for wanting the fictional Roxanne as their girlfriend. Shante recorded "Roxanne's Revenge," launching her career. Even though Roxanne Shante had nothing to do with and had no reason to take offense to the song by U.T.F.O., her response helped pave the way for the long list of "dis," or disrespectful, records that followed.

Salt 'N Pepa (sometimes spelled Salt-n-Pepa) became the first female rap stars. Rappers Salt and Pepa, along with rapper/DJ Spinderella, who joined the group after the release of its breakthrough debut album, 1986's *Hot Cool & Vicious*, had a string of hit singles that gave female rappers credibility. The dance song "Push It" became a party favorite, while "Tramp" trashed two-timing men and "I'll Take Your Man" displayed the women's seductive side. For the first time, a female rap group was respected. Writer Stephen Thomas Erlewine explains on the AllMusic (AMG) website:

As the first all-female rap crew (even their DJs were

women) of importance, the group broke down a number of doors for women in hip-hop. They were also one of the first rap artists to cross over into the pop mainstream, laying the groundwork for the music's widespread acceptance in the early '90s. Salt 'N Pepa were more pop-oriented than many of their contemporaries, since their songs were primarily party and love anthems, driven by big beats and interlaced with vaguely pro-feminist lyrics that seemed more powerful when delivered by the charismatic and sexy trio.[12]

MC Lyte, another credible female rapper, broke through in 1986 with the impassioned "I Cram to Understand U" single, which is part love song, part antidrug parable. In her subsequent material, MC Lyte raps about everything from the damaging impact of drugs and her rapping ability to having fun and being in love, showing that female rappers

Salt 'N Pepa's string of hit singles gave female rappers credibility and respect.

can rhyme about a variety of topics with lyrical skill equal to their male counterparts. "From the very beginning, I knew that there are many different sides to me," Lyte says. "In recording the very first record, it was OK to be vulnerable on record. It was OK to talk about your feelings and I just respect that in anybody in the craft that can do it. OK, you're the best at what you do and that's great, but then also have other things going on that you don't mind discussing."[13]

The Brooklyn-reared artist is the first solo female rapper to earn a gold single, for 1993's "Ruffneck." In a genre quick to dispose of its pioneers, she has maintained her status as one of the most respected female rappers of all time, a performer who is embraced for her rapping talent, not just her looks. "She's a good-looking female, don't get me wrong, but it wasn't the sex that was selling it," says platinum rapper Fabolous, who was also raised in Brooklyn. "When she got on the microphone, she was spitting like a dude, like a real MC. That definitely caught my eye back in the day."[14]

Rappers as Poets

As Run-D.M.C., LL Cool J, and female rappers earned more and more attention from newspapers and magazines that had not previously covered rap in much detail, other rappers of the golden era were becoming more and more proficient, creating increasingly complex and detailed rhymes that used complicated schemes and imagery. The artists, their followers in the streets, and even a few journalists started considering rappers poets, a step that signaled that rappers were now being taken seriously by the media. For instance, in the 1992 essay "Poets with Attitude," published in the *Washington Post*, University of Minnesota and Macalester College teacher Alexs Pate refers to specific rap songs from as early as 1987 to argue that rappers were aware of the poetic process and engaged in literary expression.

Three of the most respected rappers of this era, and the ones who arguably possessed the best poetic and storytelling abilities, were Rakim, Slick Rick, and Big Daddy Kane. Unlike most other rappers, who favored energetic deliveries, Rakim rapped in a laid-back but commanding tone that made him sound like an authoritative scholar, respected and worthy of being emulated. Rakim and his partner, DJ Eric B., released *Paid in Full*, their debut album, in 1987. The poetic power of Rakim is evident on the song "I Know You Got Soul," in which he raps about becoming one with the paper on which he writes his rhymes.

Whereas Rakim was typically serious, London-born rapper Slick Rick first garnered attention in 1985 as MC Ricky D through his work with Doug E. Fresh & the Get Fresh Crew on their songs "The Show" and "La Di Da Di," both of which feature Rick's creative storytelling ability and his humorous outlook on life. In 1988 Slick Rick released his dynamic debut album, *The Great Adventures of Slick Rick*. Resembling a series of short stories set to music, the album features Slick Rick taking listeners on journeys that are cautionary ("Children's Story"), inspirational ("Hey Young World"), and wistful ("Teenage Love"). Rick also had several sexually explicit songs that detail his relationships with women, but the racy content did not detract from Rick's storytelling skill.

Rakim had poise and Slick Rick had humor, but Big Daddy Kane was possibly the most well-rounded rapper of the golden era of rap. The Brooklyn-bred rapper established himself as a tough-talking artist whose lyrical prowess dazzled hardcore hip-hop followers and whose rugged good looks made him attractive to women. His first two albums, 1988's masterful *Long Live the Kane* and 1989's *It's a Big Daddy Thing*, showcase one of Kane's biggest strengths: his diversity. He was equally adept when rhyming about his lyrical ability ("Raw," "Ain't No Half-Steppin'"), instilling pride and hope in the hopeless ("Word to the Mother [Land]," "Another Victory"), imagining a better world ("I'll Take You There"), or seducing women ("I Get the Job Done," "Smooth Operator").

As rap journalist and editor Reginald C. Dennis wrote in the liner notes of *The Very Best of Big Daddy Kane* in 2001,

> Describing Big Daddy Kane's place in hip-hop history is like pondering the accomplishments of Miles Davis or Muhammad Ali. Both were incredibly powerful presences, even without Miles playing a note or Ali

stepping into the ring. Their energy—a near mystical aura of attraction—could be felt from a single black-and-white photograph. And in the end what they did wasn't as important as how they did it. They were just vessels for the truth—and the truth, as we all know, is magnetic. And so was Big Daddy Kane.[15]

An artist conscious that his music had an impact on his followers, Kane made a point of including political and social messages in his music, giving his poetry a purpose. "I thought that I needed to do that for the simple fact that people listened to what I say," he said. "I wasn't one of those artists where people throw my song on and just dance to it. People actually listened to the lyrics. Because of that, I thought that [having messages in my music] was something that I should get across."[16]

Rap Gets Political

Indeed, rappers during the late 1980s were mindful that their words could have an impact on their listeners. Bronx rap group Boogie Down Productions (BDP) released the confrontational *Criminal Minded* in 1987 and, after the murder of group member DJ Scott LaRock, the politically minded *By All Means Necessary* the following year. The album features powerful songs about the need for peace, the impact of political corruption, and the importance of safe sex.

BDP helped create a brand of rap later labeled "conscious rap," which incorporated political and social commentary and often advocated armed revolt against the government and other agencies that the artists considered oppressive. The movement also included Brand Nubian, X-Clan, and Poor Righteous Teachers. The most popular and arguably the most influential group of the conscious rap movement, however, was Public Enemy. After releasing the sizzling *Yo! Bum Rush the Show* in 1987, the group released, a year later, what many music critics consider the best rap album of all time, *It Takes a Nation of Millions to Hold Us Back*. As writer Stephen Thomas Erlewine writes in AllMusic:

Public Enemy rewrote the rules of hip-hop, becoming

the most influential and controversial rap group of the late '80s and, for many, the definitive rap group of all time. Building from Run-D.M.C.'s street-oriented beats and Boogie Down Productions' proto-gangsta rhyming, Public Enemy pioneered a variation of hardcore rap that was musically and politically revolutionary. With his powerful, authoritative baritone, lead rapper Chuck D rhymed about all kinds of social problems, particularly those plaguing the black community, often condoning revolutionary tactics and social activism. In the process, he directed hip-hop toward an explicitly self-aware, pro-black consciousness that became the culture's signature throughout the next decade. Musically, Public Enemy were just as revolutionary as their production team, the Bomb Squad, creating dense soundscapes that relied on avant-garde cut-and-paste techniques, unrecognizable samples, piercing sirens, relentless beats, and deep funk. It was chaotic and invigorating music, made all the more intoxicating by Chuck D's forceful vocals and the absurdist raps

Chuck D and Flavor Flav (left to right) of Public Enemy, the most influential group of the conscious rap movement, perform at the Montreux Jazz Festival in Switzerland in 1988.

of his comic foil Flavor Flav. With his comic sunglasses and an oversized clock hanging from his neck, Flav became the group's visual focal point, but he never obscured the music.[17]

The Native Tongues

Whereas Public Enemy, BDP, and others had a militaristic bent to their politically infused music, the rap collective Native Tongues (whose members included Jungle Brothers, De La Soul, A Tribe Called Quest, and Queen Latifah,

The Beastie Boys Get "Ill"

The Beastie Boys were among rap's first bad boys. Signed to the legendary Def Jam Records, the trio of Mike D, MCA, and Ad-Rock got their start in the early 1980s making punk music. But they soon turned their attention to rap, and in 1986 released their first album, the controversial and hugely successful Licensed to Ill. *Writer Stephen Thomas Erlewine explains the album's impact on www.allmusic.com:*

An amalgam of street beats, metal riffs, b-boy jokes, and satire, *Licensed to Ill* was interpreted as a mindless, obnoxious party record by many critics and conservative action groups, but that didn't stop the album from becoming the fastest-selling debut in Columbia Records' history, moving over 750,000 copies in its first six weeks. Much of that success was due to the single "Fight for Your Right (To

Party)," which became a massive crossover success. In fact, *Licensed to Ill* became the biggest-selling rap album of the '80s, which generated much criticism from certain hip-hop fans who believed that the Beasties were merely cultural pirates. On the other side of the coin, the group was being attacked from the right, who claimed their lyrics were violent and sexist and that their concerts—which featured female audience members dancing in go-go cages and a giant inflatable penis, similar to what the [rock group the Rolling] Stones used in their mid-'70s concerts—caused even more outrage. Throughout their 1987 tour, they were plagued with arrests and lawsuits, and were accused of inciting crime.

Stephen Thomas Erlewine. "Beastie Boys." AllMusic. www .allmusic.com/artist/beastie-boys-p10/biography.

among others) put more playful and inspiring but less confrontational messages in their music. The members of the collective promoted peace, justice, and equality, but their music made it clear that they were willing to enjoy themselves in the meantime.

Although each member of Native Tongues was important, De La Soul had the greatest impact on rap's development, especially with its first album, 1989's *3 Feet High and Rising*. De La Soul changed the composition of rap albums via its pioneering use of humorous skits, which were interwoven into the flow of *3 Feet High and Rising*. These skits

The Beastie Boys had the biggest-selling rap album of the 1980s with their crossover hit Licensed to Ill.

were not songs, but rather interludes that featured group members participating in a humorous game show. Today, virtually every rap album has at least one skit.

In addition to Native Tongues, other New York rap groups were making tremendous creative strides. Gang Starr, for instance, was one of the first rap groups to incorporate jazz music into its work, while Stetsasonic called itself the "hip-hop band" because it used live instruments during its recordings and performances, something unheard of in the era of sampling. The comical and controversial Beastie Boys demonstrated for the first time that white rappers could create quality rap music respected by members of the rap community. Nonetheless, Beastie Boys were treated by some critics and rap fans as a novelty act because its members were white and used juvenile humor in their music.

Rap Expands Beyond New York

White rappers were not the only ones looking to join the rap world. In the late 1980s, after the success of Run-D.M.C., LL Cool J, Salt 'N Pepa, Beastie Boys, and several movies depicting hip-hop culture, rappers from cities besides New York began making their own brand of rap music. Artists from these other cities experimented with sound, rap style, and lyrical content, continuing rap's creative development and adding new elements to the genre.

In Philadelphia, DJ Jazzy Jeff & the Fresh Prince, the good-natured rap duo whose playful songs "Parents Just Don't Understand" and "Nightmare on My Street" were quality examples of profanity-free rap, demonstrated that the genre did not have to be confrontational. In Los Angeles, King Tee delivered a California interpretation of New York's braggadocio style of rap, while MC Shy D helped put Atlanta, Georgia, on the map with his up-tempo party raps.

Each of these non–New York acts helped develop the rap scene in its own region, allowing rap to expand quickly throughout the country. With successful rappers now spread across the country, a major rap revolution was about to take place.

CHAPTER 4

Gangsta Rap

As the golden era of rap, with its celebratory, bombastic, and political emphasis, came to an end in the late 1980s, a new kind of rap was ready to take center stage. This more explicit and more profane brand of rap would become known as gangsta rap. In the early days of gangsta rap, rappers who performed it presented themselves as street documentarians, artists who reported on life in some of the roughest and poorest ghettos in America. Unlike rap from the golden era, which tended to have an optimistic, boastful bent, gangsta rap was confrontational and even scary to some listeners.

Gangsta rap featured violent lyrics along with sexually explicit themes that many critics and activists said demeaned women. It created a firestorm of controversy that led to courtroom battles and boycotts. The more explicit the material, the more attention it received.

Schoolly D Lays the Groundwork

Inspired by the gritty raps of Melle Mel on "The Message," aspiring Philadelphia rapper Schoolly D decided in the mid-1980s to take a similarly harsh approach with his music. Schoolly D made the first gangsta rap songs, profanity-filled selections in which he raps about smoking

Philadelphia rapper Schoolly D made the first gangsta rap songs.

marijuana, having sex with women, and us-ing guns.

At this time, rap was still in its developing stages and record companies were unsure of the genre's potential to sell enough units to make releasing rap albums worthwhile. Schoolly D recalls that no record companies were interested in his early music:

> I had made this demo in around '83, '84, called "Gangster Boogie." I made one pressing of it and I took it to a disc jockey by the name of Lady B. She told

Samples Bring Lawsuits

The media hype surrounding the violent lyrics of gangsta rappers and sexually explicit raps of 2 Live Crew made rap a magnet for controversy, thereby exposing the music to more listeners, some of whom purchased the music simply out of curiosity. But some of these new consumers, many of whom were older and had grown up listening to rock and roll, included listeners who had one purpose while listening to rap music: to find illegal samples contained in song.

Sampling was a simple procedure for rap producers as soon as the practice was popularized in the mid-1980s. But since sampling required using other people's music, it made rappers easy targets for copyright infringement lawsuits by the owners of the songs that were being sampled.

2 Live Crew, targeted because of the graphic sexual content of its breakthrough 1989 album, *As Nasty as They Wanna Be*, was sued by the estate of Roy Orbison over the group's usage of the music of the rock icon's song "Pretty Woman." Biz Markie, a successful, lighthearted rapper, saw his career grind to a near halt in 1991 when he was sued for sampling Gilbert O'Sullivan's "Alone Again Naturally" without permission. Biz's *I Need a Haircut* album was subsequently pulled from record stores, letting producers know that they faced a lawsuit if they sampled a song without first getting permission.

me that no record company was going to sign it because I was talking about weed [marijuana] and guns. After that, I knew that nobody was going to sign it. So I thought that if [rap businessman] Russell Simmons was a rapper, he'd do his own label. And he said [in an interview] that, "If I was a rapper like my brother [Run-D.M.C.'s Run], I would just do my own label." So I just said, "[I'll do it myself]." They didn't even want to hear clean rap, so I just started doing little things here and there to save up the money to press up my own records. I was part of a [local rap] crew anyway, so I knew everybody in every [Philadelphia record] shop, like Funk of Martin, Sound of Market. All the record stores said that if I pressed the record up, they'd sell them. So I did it.[18]

Launched in 1983, his Schoolly D Records was the first artist-owned rap label. In the next few years Schoolly D enjoyed regional, but not national, success. His hits included the thunderous "P.S.K. 'What Does It Mean'?" about his Philadelphia gang of violent friends, and the story-driven "Saturday Night" about his wild, violent sexual adventures on Saturday nights. After Schoolly D became an underground sensation, Jive Records signed him to a recording contract and released several of his albums.

As Schoolly D was becoming one of the most talked-about rappers in the streets of Philadelphia, rappers from other cities started making equally controversial and abrasive music. Oakland, California, rapper Too $hort reported on the lifestyle of pimps and prostitutes over slow, bass-heavy music; Los Angeles rappers Ice-T and Toddy Tee rapped about the violent, gang-infested streets of their city over spare beats; and the Houston, Texas, collective Geto Boys brought vivid violence to the forefront with its aggressive productions. In New York, rapper Just Ice and rap duo Boogie Down Productions were also releasing music with violent overtones that included explicit lyrics about sex and drugs.

Straight Outta Compton Makes a Mark

As gangsta rap was gaining momentum, Eazy-E and N.W.A appeared with music that would galvanize the rap world. Eric "Eazy-E" Wright was a small-time drug dealer and aspiring record executive who revolutionized both the rap record business and the lyrical direction of the music with releases from his record company, whose roster included Eazy-E himself and his flagship group N.W.A, whose other members were Dr. Dre, Ice Cube, MC Ren, and DJ Yella.

The first Eazy-E album, *Eazy Duz It*, and the first N.W.A album, *Straight Outta Compton*, both released in 1988, were full of profanity and got virtually no radio or video play. With violent, jarring music that contained an unprecedented combination of humor, misogyny, and political insight, N.W.A rapped in explicit and articulate terms about the violence and drugs consuming its California communities. According to the *Washington Post*, they "weren't the first rappers to do songs about crime, guns and gang violence, but they heightened the mayhem and the profanity to an unprecedented, nearly surreal degree."[19]

Gangsta Rap Gets Attacked

As exciting as its music may have been, N.W.A also made a mark by berating the police for abusing innocent blacks in the ghetto on *Straight Outta Compton*. Law enforcement officials did not appreciate the antagonistic material. In 1989 N.W.A received a now-famous letter from the FBI warning it against releasing songs that advocated violence against law enforcement, while a number of police organizations decided not to provide security at N.W.A performances. The members of N.W.A were arrested and later acquitted of obscenity charges in Cincinnati, Ohio, and had their albums seized in England because they were deemed obscene.

The controversy, along with a string of brilliant but brutal albums, drew fans to the music of Eazy-E and N.W.A, which was more polished and accessible than that of earlier gangsta rappers thanks to the crisp, driving production from Dr. Dre and DJ Yella. Their violent music and public appearances catapulted Eazy-E and N.W.A to rap superstardom.

The Geto Boys was another gangsta rap act that was targeted because of its violent lyrics. The release of the Houston group's self-titled 1990 album was delayed when Geffen Records decided not to distribute the record, claiming it glamorized violence and graphic sexual imagery. Soon after, Geffen Records terminated its agreement with subsidiary Def American Records, which had signed the Geto Boys, citing a growing difference in creative philosophy.

In addition to enduring the wrath of law enforcement agencies and record labels unwilling to release potentially controversial material, gangsta rappers found themselves

MC Ren and Eazy-E (left to right) from N.W.A perform in Kansas City, Missouri, in 1989 during their Straight Outta Compton *tour. The album—especially its lyrics critical of police tactics—generated a lot of controversy.*

under attack from journalists, who criticized the celebratory, one-sided view of violence that gangsta rap portrayed. In an article titled "Rap's Hostile Fringe," *Washington Post* writer David Mills explains how the music of gangsta rappers failed to provide an even, realistic portrayal of violence in the streets:

> The hard-core street rappers defend their violent lyrics as a reflection of "reality." But for all the gunshots they mix into their music, rappers rarely try to dramatize that reality—a young man flat on the ground, a knot of lead in his chest, pleading as death slowly takes him in. It's easier for them to imagine themselves pulling the trigger.[20]

Other writers noted that the animosity toward women and the rationale for the violence depicted in the lyrics of

Body Count Controversy

With N.W.A, 2 Live Crew, and the Geto Boys drawing the ire of the police and political activists, it was clear rap music was a target. Rap was such a polarizing topic, in fact, that another controversy linked to rap was actually caused by a song recorded by a rock-and-roll group.

In 1992 Ice-T created this major controversy with the song "Cop Killer" by his offshoot rock group Body Count. The song, which Ice-T sang from the perspective of someone who kills police officers, was protested by police activist organizations. Even though Ice-T shouted and sang his lyrics and did not rap them, he and the entire rap genre were blamed for advocating violence against law enforcement. Writer Stephen Thomas Erlewine

explains in his biography of Ice-T on the AllMusic website:

> *Body Count* proved to be a major turning point in Ice-T's career. On the basis of the track "Cop Killer"— where he sang from the point-of-view of a police murderer—the record ignited a national controversy; it was protested by the NRA [National Rifle Association] and police activist groups. Time Warner Records initially supported Ice-T, yet they refused to release his new rap album, *Home Invasion*, on the basis of the record cover. Ice-T and the label parted ways by the end of the year.

Stephen Thomas Erlewine. "Ice-T." AllMusic. www.all music.com/artist/ice-t-p89063/biography.

gangsta rap songs were becoming increasingly sensational and without political overtones. *Baltimore Sun* pop music critic J.D. Considine wrote, "It's hard to excuse raps that present women not as people but as orifices, that offer gunplay and physical violence not as a fact of life but as a viable means of settling scores, and that suggest that attitude is a reasonable compensation for a sense of self-worth."[21]

Gangsta Rap as Expression

One of the most common accusations leveled at gangsta rap was that it would encourage people to commit violence. Rappers did not agree, arguing instead that their music was a crucial expression of pain and outrage. "A record can't make nobody do anything," N.W.A's MC Ren told *Newsweek* in 1991. "Sometimes doing a record is just my way of getting back, 'cause when [police] got you jacked up on a car, and they got a gun to your head, you can't say s---. Doing records I can speak out. When people listen to the record, that's their way of speaking back."[22]

Another rapper who "spoke out" through his music was Ice Cube, who left N.W.A and started a solo career in 1990. His work often depicted the pain caused by society's seeming indifference to the suffering of blacks in ghettos across America. In his review of Ice Cube's *AmeriKKKa's Most Wanted*, the *Washington Post*'s David Mills noted, "After the mad burst of gunshots in the one-minute drama 'The Drive-By,' the voice of a newscaster is heard: 'Outside of the South-Central area, few cared about the violence because it didn't affect them.' Ice Cube clearly wants to be more than scandalous."[23]

As time went on and the shock value of gangsta rap began to fade, more people began to understand the political messages sometimes contained in the music. In fact, some music critics began to write about the prophetic properties of gangsta rap. Several critics noticed that the rage and sense of injustice contained in the work of N.W.A foretold the riots that ensued after four white police officers were acquitted in the videotaped beating of black Los Angeles motorist Rodney King. The *Washington Post* staff writer Richard Harrington, for instance, wrote, "In the wake of the Los Angeles riots, the media belatedly recognized that rap, in the tradition of vanguard political art, had for several years provided an early warning system that didn't wake up a slumbering and inattentive bureaucracy until it was too late."[24]

LL Cool J, one the most respected members of the hip-hop community, also recognized the significance of gangsta rappers:

I listen to the politicians and activists blame rap for everything under the sun, from world violence to world hunger. But if you removed every rapper from the face

---

Ice Cube's music spoke out about the suffering of blacks in ghettos across America.

of the earth, you'd still have violence and wars. In fact, if not for certain rappers, "mainstream" society would have no idea of what is going on in our communities, where real war is being waged every day. For many Americans, life is rough, and gangsta rap was born out of that misery, pain, and hunger. It didn't create it.[25]

California Becomes a Hip-Hop Hotbed

But gangsta rap did create something significant: a new business opportunity for gangsta rappers. The success of Eazy-E and N.W.A had record labels scrambling to find their own gangsta rappers and led to a wave of artists from

Pop Rap from L.A.

Even though Los Angeles gangsta rappers were the obvious beneficiaries of the success of Eazy-E and N.W.A, the momentum created by their popularity also allowed other, non-gangster Los Angeles rap acts to earn a chance in the spotlight. Pop rapper Tone-Loc broke through in 1989 with his infectious smash singles "Wild Thing" and "Funky Cold Medina," two catchy tunes that contain a winning mix of captivating plotlines and humor. Soon thereafter, Young MC, who wrote lyrics for Tone-Loc, scored his own hits with the party song "Bust A Move" and the humorous look at school mischief, "Principal's Office."

Even though Tone-Loc and Young MC were quality artists with solid albums, they were considered by the rap industry as pop acts who were only novelties and not true representations of what rap was really about: the streets that gangsta rap portrayed.

As writer Stephen Thomas Erlewine explains in his review of Young MC's *Stone Cold Rhymin'* album on the AllMusic website,

Young MC wasn't given props [respect] at the time and he wasn't respected in the years following the release of his debut *Stone Cold Rhymin'*, largely because he worked entirely in the pop-rap/crossover vein. All the same, that's what's great about his debut, since it's exceptionally clever and effective, a wonderful combination of deft rhymes and skillful production.

Stephen Thomas Erlewine. "Stone Cold Rhymin' (Deluxe Edition)." AllMusic. www.allmusic.com/album/stone -cold-rhymin-deluxe-edition-r1615251.

Compton, the tough Los Angeles suburb that N.W.A put on the national radar. After N.W.A came Compton acts DJ Quik and Compton's Most Wanted.

A multitude of other talented, gangster-inspired rap groups from Los Angeles, including the smooth Above the Law, the political WC and the MAAD Circle, and the pro-marijuana Cypress Hill, soon became hugely successful as they focused on the harsh reality that ghetto residents often faced. Suddenly, profanity, violence, and sex were what the record companies clamored for, helping make gangsta rap the most popular and promoted style of rap.

Even though this new wave of California gangsta rap acts was celebrated by rap fans, detractors viewed the groups as exploitative. "One group dares to call itself Compton's Most Wanted, capitalizing on that area's reputation for gang violence, a reputation made international by N.W.A's platinum album [*Straight Outta Compton*],"[26] David Mills wrote.

Gangsta Rap's New Sound

The tension that gangsta rap depicted soon appeared within gangsta rap groups themselves. Ice Cube left Eazy-E's company in 1989 because of a financial dispute. Dr. Dre later departed Eazy-E, also over money issues. In early 1992 Dr. Dre released "Deep Cover," a single from the soundtrack of the movie of the same name that introduced new Dr. Dre protégé Snoop Doggy Dogg, who also rapped on the song.

Snoop Doggy Dogg (known today as Snoop Dogg) was a lanky, laid-back rapper from the Los Angeles suburb of Long Beach. His slick raps and relaxed rhyme style struck a chord with rap fans. The release of "Deep Cover" established Snoop Dogg as a promising new talent and signaled the triumphant return of Dr. Dre. But it was the release of the first Dr. Dre solo album, *The Chronic*, at the end of 1992 that made both Dr. Dre and Snoop Dogg, who was featured prominently on the album, superstars.

Whereas the music Dr. Dre produced for N.W.A is simmering with rage, the music on *The Chronic* contains a heavy funk influence, which results in a more relaxed musical sound that is easier for a wider range of people to digest.

Still, however, the lyrics written by Dr. Dre, Snoop Dogg, and other guests, including future rap stars Kurupt and Daz Dillinger, contain the same type of violent imagery and profanity that just a few years before had bothered governmental agencies, music critics, and fans.

Thanks in part to the censorship battles and critical backlash N.W.A and the Geto Boys faced, Dr. Dre and *The Chronic* were not met with the kind of heated, repeated protests that earlier gangsta rap was. Those battles had already run their course, clearing the way for mainstream outlets such as *Rolling Stone* magazine and MTV to embrace gangsta rap as a form of legitimate music.

This acceptance was a turning point for rap. For the first time, rap music commanded attention because of the quality of the music and not because it was a fad, a gimmick, or something controversial. In fact, in 1997 *Rolling Stone,* considered the premier rock-and-roll magazine, listed *The Chronic* as one of the two hundred albums on its Essential Rock Collection list. In the review of the album that accompanied the list, music critic Lorraine Ali said, "*The Chronic* changed the sound of hip-hop and R&B, and its effects, both positive and negative, resonate through '90s pop culture."[27]

2 Live Crew Gets *Nasty*

While N.W.A, Snoop Dogg, the Geto Boys, and other rap groups took violence as their theme, 2 Live Crew created controversy by rapping about sex in explicit terms. The group recorded dozens of songs that contained profane descriptions of sex acts. In 1990 the Miami, Florida, rap

2 Live Crew's records contain sexually explicit lyrics, causing many stores to pull them from shelves. The group's t-shirts at the 1989 MTV Video Music Awards address censorship of their records.

group's *As Nasty as They Wanna Be* album, its third, was pulled from record store shelves in several states, including Florida and Maryland, after government officials asked retailers to restrict sales of the album to adults. Some record stores then went a step further by removing all 2 Live Crew recordings from their stores.

In June 1990 a U.S. District Court judge in Florida ruled that *As Nasty as They Wanna Be* was obscene, and two of the four members of 2 Live Crew were arrested after performing songs deemed obscene. However, in October 1990 a Florida jury, claiming to view the lyrics as art, acquitted 2 Live Crew of performing obscene material. The case drew national attention to the legal debate about freedom of speech and the difficulty of defining what is and is not deemed obscene.

National publications covered the 2 Live Crew obscenity trial, and once it was over, some people defended the group's music. "Clearly this judgment should serve as notice to others trying to find music obscene that Americans believe very strongly in our First Amendment rights," Trish Heimers, speaking on behalf of the Recording Industry Association of America, told the *Washington Post*. "Whether they find it vulgar or obnoxious or lewd still does not mean that it is criminally obscene."[28] Other commentators, however, took a harsher view. *Washington Post* columnist Jonathan Yardley wrote,

> The recording is filth, pure and simple, utterly devoid of socially or artistically redeeming qualities. "As Nasty as They Wanna Be" is to all intents and purposes one uninterrupted barrage of lewd and scatological language, a monotonous recitation of all the standard-issue four-letter words and numerous others of greater length; it is—yes—witless, strident, insulting to even the dullest intelligence and, above all else, contemptuous of women. It is beyond the powers of my imagination to conceive that it could bring pleasure to anyone, though apparently it does.[29]

New York Embraces Gangsta Rap

N.W.A, 2 Live Crew, and Dr. Dre earned as much media exposure as rap had ever experienced to this point, if not more, yet the rest of the rap community was not necessarily happy about the rise of the gangsta rap scene, especially in Los Angeles. New York rappers initially dismissed the gangsta rap of the West Coast as unimaginative, pointless, and not "real" hip-hop because it lacked the lyrical complexity that had blossomed during the golden era of rap. New York rapper Tim Dog even recorded a song criticizing the entire city of Compton and dedicated his debut album, 1991's *Penicillin on Wax*, to attacking the artistic merit of Los Angeles–based rappers.

Still, as Eazy-E, Dr. Dre, Snoop Dogg, and other rappers became more popular than any other rap acts, their style influenced a legion of New York rappers, including Kool G. Rap & DJ Polo, the Beatnuts, Mobb Deep, and Fat Joe, all of whom infused their music with a gritty feel that showed the direct influence of the confrontational material of Eazy-E and N.W.A. Even so, East Coast rap's distaste for the rapid rise of the West Coast led to an understated bitterness between the two primary rap cities. New Yorkers did not view the West Coast artists as legitimate, and the Los Angeles artists resented this lack of respect. The competition led to an explosion of rap as a business.

CHAPTER 5

Rap Business Explodes

As rap's popularity and cultural influence continued to expand in the early 1990s, rap music became increasingly controversial and violent. But another crucial development was also taking place: The rise of gangsta rap created a new generation of artists who became astute businessmen. They started their own record companies and had the power to sign artists and dictate how money was going to be spent to promote them, making rap's financial stakes bigger than ever.

Eazy-E Changes the Rap Business Model

Like Schoolly D before him, Eazy-E decided to start his own record company in the 1980s. His Ruthless Records released a few singles through local record distributors and enjoyed modest success, but Eazy-E wanted national exposure. A visionary who dreamed of becoming a music industry mogul, he had no interest in running a record company whose artists were popular only in Southern California. He and his manager started shopping his music and that of N.W.A to major record labels.

Eazy-E was rejected by several of these labels, which were not interested in doing business with an unproven rap record executive. But Priority Records, an independent com-

Eazy-E and N.W.A created a style that became identifiable as West Coast rap.

pany that had released a number of rap compilations, was interested in the graphic, shocking music that Eazy-E and N.W.A recorded. So, at a time when no rap artist from the West Coast had made a national impact, Ruthless Records signed a production deal with Priority Records for albums from these rappers. Ruthless had to deliver albums from N.W.A and Eazy-E, and Priority was responsible for the distribution of those records and the implementation of Ruthless' marketing plan, which included pushing the potentially frightening image that Eazy-E and N.W.A had guns and were not afraid to use them.

The rest of the imagery N.W.A used was equally important, as it created a style that was easily identified as that of West Coast rappers. The members of N.W.A often wore dark sunglasses (which Eazy-E later sold through order forms in Ruthless Records albums) and all-black clothing featuring the logos of the Los Angeles Raiders and Los Angeles Kings sports teams. Eazy-E and Ice Cube also wore Jheri curls, a hairstyle popular among black men in Los Angeles that was identified by loose curls and a shiny appearance.

Like Run-D.M.C. before them, the N.W.A rappers inspired a generation of kids to follow their fashion lead. Los Angeles radio personality Julio G explains the appeal of Eazy-E:

> He was really that street person that people relate to because everybody knows a guy like him. In the hood, everybody knows that dude. Even when you look at his pictures, it just signifies and shows you a lifestyle and an era of Los Angeles that he represented. He represented a lot of people that were like that with the jheri curl and the hat.[30]

Even though Ruthless and Priority Records had little music industry muscle, once Eazy-E and N.W.A were promoted nationally, both their music and their look become wildly popular. Eazy-E's *Eazy Duz It* and N.W.A's *Straight Outta Compton* sold more than a million copies each. At the time, that was an astronomically high figure for an independently released rap album.

Ruthless Sets a Precedent

Virtually overnight, rappers became more than artists: They became businessmen who controlled the direction and vision of the music and the artists who recorded for their companies. "What Rosa Parks did for the civil rights movement, Eazy-E did for hip-hop," says Phyllis Pollack, a publicist who represented Eazy-E and some of the artists at his Ruthless Records. "He kicked the door open. I know right now everybody claims to have a label, but Eric was the first hip-hop artist to really make this work on the level that he did."[31]

Rap artists, often looked down upon by corporations and executives who did not view rap as music, could now put their records out themselves, market themselves as they saw fit, and still sell millions of copies, as Eazy-E had demonstrated. "He made a mark and set a blueprint for people to follow in the business," says Eazy's widow, Tomica Wright,

Bone Resurrects Ruthless

As Death Row Records became the prominent West Coast rap label, Eazy-E and his Ruthless Records faded from the spotlight. Eazy-E rebounded by branching out of Southern California and signing Cleveland, Ohio, rap group Bone Thugs-N-Harmony, who popularized the tongue-twisting rap style introduced in the early 1990s by Twista, then known as Tung Twista. Below is an excerpt from www.allmusic.com's biography of the group:

Graced with a quick, sometimes sung delivery, Bone Thugs-N-Harmony burst out of the Midwest in the mid-'90s with a pair of massive hits ("Thuggish Ruggish Bone" and "Tha Crossroads") along with a great album (*E 1999 Eternal*) and then quickly unraveled. Eazy-E signed the group—initially comprised of Krayzie Bone, Wish Bone, Flesh-N-Bone, Layzie Bone, and Bizzy Bone—to Ruthless Records and released a debut EP [extended play], *Creepin on ah Come Up* (1994). The EP boasted "Thuggish Ruggish Bone," a conventional G-funk song with an unconventional array of Bone Thug rappers that became an overnight summer anthem, especially throughout the Midwest. Amid the fervor, the Cleveland rap group entered the studio immediately and emerged with a remarkable album, *E 1999 Eternal* (1995). The album topped the charts and spawned a pair of popular singles, "1st of the Month" and "Tha Crossroads," the latter a Grammy Award recipient. . . . As was in vogue at the time, the group members pursued respective solo careers and also a Mo Thugs Family spinoff group.

Jason Birchmeier. "Bone Thugs-N-Harmony." AllMusic. www.allmusic.com/artist/bone-thugs-n-harmony-p44741.

who today runs Ruthless Records. "He took something that was looked upon in a negative sense, invested money in the idea and brought it to where people paid attention and wanted to listen to what he and his [artists] had to say."[32]

The success of the Eazy-E and N.W.A albums indeed changed the music community's mind, and Eazy-E soon signed distribution deals for his other artists with a variety of record companies, including major ones such as Atlantic and Epic. The success of Ruthless Records made an impression on a generation of future rappers. Layzie Bone, a member of the multiplatinum and Grammy Award–winning rap group Bone Thugs-N-Harmony, was signed to Ruthless. Layzie Bone, who with Bone Thugs-N-Harmony has its own Mo Thugs Records label, recalls,

> He showed us that you can be more than just a rapper. If it wasn't for Eazy-E, there probably wouldn't have been any Master Ps [the rapper whose No Limit Records was among the most successful rap record companies in the late 1990s] or Roc-A-Fellas [the company cofounded by Jay-Z]. All of them are patterned off of what Eazy-E did. He showed them everything, how to own your masters, be in control of your company and get the bulk of your money. He showed us how to be executives and really get paid as opposed to being [just] an artist. He really started the real level of taking an independent major.[33]

Rappers Transition to Movies

By focusing on their business as much as their music, many rappers began realizing their moneymaking potential. Appearing in a movie or a commercial, for instance, was widely seen as selling out in the first decade or so of recorded rap music, as the movies and commercials of that time typically cast rappers in shallow, stereotypical roles. But both business-minded rappers looking to increase their exposure (and bank accounts) and movie studios looking for new ways to attract people to movie theaters realized in the early 1990s that rappers could be major box office draws.

Almost a decade after the release of such rap-inclusive films as *Flashdance* and *Breakin'*, the movie studios started casting rappers, most of whom had no formal acting training or experience, in leading roles for major motion pictures. Most of these films and television programs featured rappers in roles that required little acting and for the most part mirrored their rapping personas. Lighthearted duo Kid 'N Play launched the successful *House Party* franchise in 1990. Ice-T, who appeared in *Breakin'* in 1984, scored a starring role as a police officer in *New Jack City*, an acclaimed film that also features cameos from hip-hop figures such as Flavor Flav and Fab Five Freddy. In it, Ice-T infused his character with a toughness and swagger that matched his recording personality. Ice Cube also made a successful transition into film with the acclaimed *Boyz N the Hood* in 1991, playing an inner-city Los Angeles teen lured by the guns and violence surrounding him.

Will Smith, better known then by his rap name the Fresh Prince, became a television star in 1990 thanks to his leading role in *The Fresh Prince of Bel-Air*. In the show, Smith played a fun-loving, mischievous teen who moves to the affluent Los Angeles suburb of Bel-Air to avoid the pitfalls and temptations of his native Philadelphia streets. Smith, however, took a major gamble in 1993 when he portrayed a gay hustler who befriends a rich white couple in the movie *Six Degrees of Separation*. The impressive performance helped establish Smith as a credible actor and led to his being cast in the 1995 action film *Bad Boys* with comedian Martin Lawrence and the 1996 action blockbuster *Independence Day*, which catapulted him to movie superstardom.

Actor and rapper Will Smith outside the studios where his 1990s hit TV series The Fresh Prince of Bel-Air *was filmed.*

Rap Tours Emerge

Rappers began touring in the early 1980s, but the growth of the rap touring business lagged behind the explosion of record sales of rap albums throughout the 1980s and 1990s. With notable exceptions such as the Fresh Fest Tour, rap tours in the 1980s and throughout much of the 1990s were limited, in part, because of the violence associated with rap. In 1986, for instance, there was a riot at a Run-D.M.C. concert in Long Beach, California, before Run-D.M.C. appeared onstage.

Rap tours started gaining credibility in 1999 thanks in large part to the Hard Knock Life Tour, which Jay-Z headlined and which was the first rap tour in a decade to play in arenas. Building on that success, independent rappers such as Tech N9ne and Murs developed solid fan bases by touring the United States and abroad, often performing more than two hundred times a year. Tech N9ne explains that his fans enjoy the professionalism of his concerts: "I'm blessed because some people cannot do it in a way that you would want to go see them more than once. People say they keep coming back and they [tell their friends], 'You've got to see this.'"

Tech N9ne, phone interview with the author, May 20, 2011.

Death Row Records Emerges

With many rappers selling millions of albums with their own companies and others gradually becoming box office stars, the stage was set for a rap company to become one of the most dominant forces in the popular music business. The creative force behind this new company already had a history of making provocative, popular music.

In 1991 bodyguard and aspiring music industry mogul Marion "Suge" Knight, reportedly through threats of violence, got Dr. Dre out of his recording contract with Eazy-E and Ruthless Records. Knight and Dr. Dre teamed to form their own company, Death Row Records, which released Dr. Dre's solo album, *The Chronic*, in 1992.

The success of the album established Death Row Records as one of the most powerful rap record companies in the country. The next Death Row Records release was *Doggystyle*, the first album from Snoop Dogg. It debuted as the number-one album in the country upon its release in 1993, making Snoop Dogg the first new artist ever to have an album enter the pop music charts at number one. After fewer than two years in business, Death Row Records thus had the respect of the music industry and the best-selling album in the nation.

Bad Boy Entertainment Is Born

While Death Row Records was dominating the rap market, New Yorker Sean "Puffy" Combs (today known as Diddy) was making plans to enter the rap world as a label head, too. An established music producer, Combs formed Bad Boy Entertainment in 1993 and landed a distribution deal with industry powerhouse Arista Records. The deal ensured that all Bad Boy releases would be available at record stores worldwide.

The next year, Bad Boy Entertainment became an industry powerhouse itself when it released the epic debut album *Ready to Die* by the Notorious B.I.G. Formerly known as Biggie Smalls, the stocky Brooklynite possessed tremendous rapping skill. His wordplay was witty, his vocabulary was vast, his delivery was flawless, his timing was impeccable, his voice was commanding, and his song concepts were innovative. *Ready to Die* made perfect use of all of these talents and gave New Yorkers a gangsta rapper from their own area to champion.

Equally important was that *Ready to Die* was a New York (or East Coast) interpretation of gangsta rap. Unlike most East Coast rappers before him, B.I.G. infused his music with the edge, paranoia, and rage that filled the best gangsta rap albums. As a storyteller, B.I.G. depicted himself in a variety of volatile situations, making his album a journey through the New York rap underworld, just as Eazy-E and N.W.A

Sean "Puffy" Combs formed Bad Boy Entertainment in 1993 and became an industry powerhouse.

had taken listeners on similar trips through Los Angeles a few years earlier.

In "Warning," for example, B.I.G. raps about being hunted down for his wealth, while on "Gimme the Loot" he is the one doing the robbing. "Juicy" documents his rise from average ghetto resident to hip-hop star, and in "One

More Chance" he boasts in a devilishly clever manner about his sexual prowess and his ability to juggle relationships with a number of women. On "Big Poppa," B.I.G. raps over a smooth, keyboard-driven beat that has the same slow, relaxed feel of much of the Los Angeles rap of the time. By contrast, New York rap generally featured heavy drum patterns, braggadocio rhymes, and aggressive delivery styles.

Rivalry Between Death Row and Bad Boy

The differences between New York and Los Angeles rap became a point of contention among rap fans. Furthermore, with rap releases now regularly debuting as the number-one album in the country and rap albums routinely selling mil-

Rap Magazines Create Controversy

In November 1994 2Pac was shot five times (and survived) in an apparent robbery attempt in the lobby of Times Square's Quad Recording Studios in New York. At the time, mainstream media was still relatively reluctant to give rap much coverage, so hip-hop periodicals, notably *Vibe* and *The Source*, ran with the story. In a series of back-and-forth exchanges, conveniently spread from one issue to the next, urban music magazines fanned the flames that would set the stage for what would eventually be the East Coast/West Coast rap beef.

In the April 1995 issue of *Vibe*, 2Pac accused his former friend the Notorious B.I.G., Bad Boy founder Sean "P. Diddy" Combs, and others of coordinating his shooting at the New York studio. Although *Vibe* did not get in touch with B.I.G. for comment in the issue—2Pac was making slanderous statements that did not seem to be corroborated by any research or secondary follow-up—they did catch up with him in enough time to put him on a cover of his own, this time without input from 2Pac, who was suddenly unavailable.

2Pac was trying to diffuse the growing East Coast/West Coast beef in his own way. In addition to singling out the people he had problems with on his incendiary "Hit 'Em Up," the rapper was also working on the *One Nation* album with a number of East Coast rappers, including Big Daddy Kane and Nice & Smooth, in an attempt to show that his problems were with specific individuals, not an entire region. The rap media, though, did not run with that story.

lions of copies, rap became the focus of an unprecedented amount of media coverage. To many of those in the rap community, the attention meant that the stakes were higher and that they would do whatever was necessary to be considered the best. Rap had become more than just music or a way for people to express themselves. It was now big business, requiring a constant struggle by the artists and the companies to which they were signed to stay at the top.

The two rap labels earning most of the accolades during this period were Death Row Records and Bad Boy Entertainment. In 1995 a rivalry between the two companies—and eventually between the West Coast and East Coast styles of rap—was officially born.

At the Source Awards, an event held in New York by the industry-leading publication to celebrate rap, Death Row's Suge Knight addressed the audience, several of whom were rap artists. He urged rappers and singers who did not want company CEOs appearing on their songs and in their videos to sign with Death Row Records. The comments were aimed at Bad Boy's Diddy, who was getting a reputation for appearing on songs and in videos of his artists. Diddy was criticized for this because it appeared as though he was trying to steal the spotlight for himself. When he appeared onstage later in the show, Diddy downplayed any animosity Knight intended. Nonetheless, in a show of support for the East Coast, the New York crowd later booed Death Row's Snoop Dogg, who felt disrespected by the outpouring of hostility. The fallout from this event led to a deadly rap rivalry.

2Pac Joins Death Row Records

With tension building between Death Row Records and Bad Boy Entertainment, and between East Coast and West Coast rappers, Death Row Records added a controversial West Coast artist to its roster. Embattled rap star 2Pac, who had released three hit albums and also delivered acclaimed appearances in a number of films, was serving time in prison for sexual assault. Eager to regain his freedom, 2Pac agreed to sign to Death Row Records in 1995 if it would expedite his release from prison. Death Row obliged, and overnight 2Pac became the star of the label.

2Pac had been shot in a New York recording studio in 1994 and survived. In a series of interviews with the national media, he accused both Diddy and the Notorious B.I.G. of involvement in the shooting. 2Pac's accusations further strained the already tenuous relationship between Bad Boy and Death Row artists and established 2Pac as a star who was willing to speak his mind, regardless of whom he might offend and regardless of the consequences.

Like his public statements, 2Pac's music was equally noteworthy. He rapped freely about things that made him

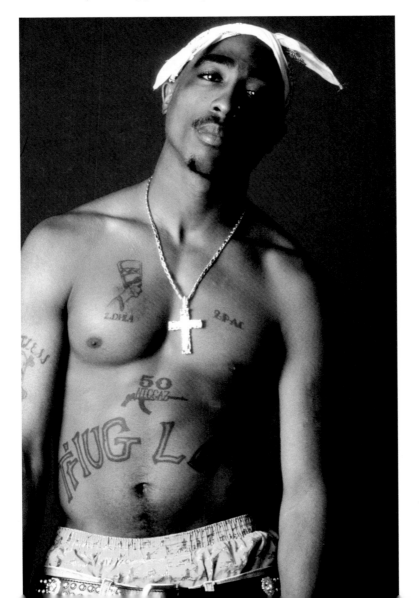

2Pac became the model for how rappers were supposed to act and look, taking cues from Los Angeles gang members.

happy, sad, and upset, often in profane outbursts followed by thoughtful reflection. 2Pac was a performer that many fans could identify with because of his willingness to share his pain and confusion. He did not put himself above his followers. Instead, he was just like them, struggling to find his way in an increasingly complicated world. Young Noble, a friend of 2Pac's and a member of the rap group Outlawz, explains how he and his group have been influenced by 2Pac:

> He was our teacher as far as all this [the music business]. We watched him. We'd be on the way to the studio and there'd be something that would happen and he's putting it in a rap, right there on the spot. To me, that's what music is about, experience. When you make music like that, it lasts forever. That's why some people would rather listen to some oldies than what's out now. It's timeless when it comes from the heart if you do it right. We're trying to make music like that.[34]

As important as 2Pac's music was, he also changed rap in other ways. Through his aggressive videos, 2Pac became the model for what a rapper was supposed to act and look like. 2Pac's music became, in effect, secondary to his celebrity and his image.

That image included acting like a thug (a term 2Pac applied to himself) and wearing bandannas, something Los Angeles gang members were also famous for doing.

2Pac, already upset with the Notorious B.I.G. and Diddy, was more than happy to oblige when Suge Knight asked him to berate both B.I.G. and Diddy at every opportunity. This allowed him to release the rage he felt toward them, and also earned him millions of followers.

2Pac Wages War

In the fall of 1995 2Pac released the single "California Love," a duet with Dr. Dre that marked 2Pac's first release on Death Row Records. The song quickly became the biggest rap song of the season and set the stage for the February 1996 release of his first Death Row Records release, the double album *All Eyez on Me*.

But it was the 2Pac single "Hit 'Em Up" that had music fans in a frenzy. In this confrontational tune, 2Pac levels bone-crushing insults at B.I.G. and the rest of the Bad Boy roster, claiming, among other things, that he had had sex with B.I.G.'s wife. 2Pac also passed the microphone to his friends the Outlawz, who in turn proceeded to vocally pummel B.I.G. and his crew. "Hit 'Em Up" stands as one of the most stinging songs in rap history and certainly one of the most popular.

But as Death Row became more popular and embraced violence, it lost its creative musical edge. Dr. Dre, for one, did not condone the increasingly hostile Death Row environment and later in 1996 he left the label he had cofounded. 2Pac was not able to leave the label on his own terms. At the peak of his rivalry with B.I.G. and Bad Boy, 2Pac was shot and killed in Las Vegas, Nevada, in September 1996. The murder remains unsolved.

Just six months after 2Pac's death, the Notorious B.I.G. was shot to death in Los Angeles.

The deaths of 2Pac and the Notorious B.I.G. put a dark cloud over the hip-hop industry. With these murders, rap had gone from reporting about violence in the early days of gangsta rap to creating and becoming part of the violence itself. Nonetheless, the increasing success of rap music gave a multitude of artists across the country hope that they could become rap's next stars.

CHAPTER 6

Rise of the South and of the DJ

I n the spring of 1997 rap was reeling from the loss of two of its biggest stars, 2Pac and the Notorious B.I.G. The deaths of these two artists brought gangsta rap an abundance of notoriety. The genre was again viewed by media pundits as an exclusively negative form of music, and some record companies looked to sign safer, less confrontational artists. One by-product of this shift in attitude was a new focus on two other groups of hip-hoppers: Southern rappers and DJs.

Both rappers from the South (and to a lesser degree from the Midwest) and DJs had been marginalized by rappers in New York and Los Angeles and the major recording companies located in these cities. Nonetheless, they had developed their own followings, with different levels of success. The South became the hottest breeding ground for rap in the mid- and late 1990s, while DJs developed a sizable following for their own work.

The Rise of Southern and Midwestern Rap

As rap emerged as a cultural power, more people wanted to participate. For a three- or four-year period beginning in about 1995, artists with divergent sounds and lyrical approaches started making rap music in such cities as Atlanta,

Georgia; Memphis, Tennessee; Houston, Texas; and New Orleans, Louisiana. In each city a specific and identifiable sound emerged that was distinguishable from the rap music coming from other cities. These distinguishing sounds led to an increasing regionalism in rap, as many fans stopped listening to music from other areas and supported artists from their own city, who used the same slang and rapped about local issues that mattered to them.

For example, the Southern artists in particular rhymed over either energetic beats or beats that used the same soulful feel as the music used in 1970s blaxploitation films. (These low-budget films featured predominantly black casts at a time when blacks had few roles in major motion pictures.) Southern rappers also expanded the types of deliveries that rappers employed and the nuances of the raps themselves. OutKast, for instance, did not hide its Southern twang in its raps, as other Southern rappers had done before.

Indeed, a pivotal release for Southern rap was *Southernplayalisticadillacmuzik*, the 1994 debut album from OutKast, the Atlanta duo consisting of Andre 3000 (also known as Dre) and Big Boi. The album resonated because for one of the first times in rap history, a rap act from the South did not copy or imitate the sound and style of established rappers from the East or West. Rather, the duo embraced their Atlanta roots, used Southern slang in their raps, and rapped about the black experience in the South. Bubba Sparxxx, a rapper from rural Georgia, remembers the impact *Southernplayalisticadillacmuzik* had on his life:

It inspired me when I heard *Southernplayalisticadillacmuzik*. . . . Those were Southern Black boys, like the kind I went to school with, the kind I knew, the kind my closest neighbor was. They were people that talked like me, they were like people I played football with. So I could just relate more to that story. I had dabbled around writing raps, and I was like 16 or 17, and I said, I really think I can do this.[35]

Other rappers also saw the South as a fertile ground for new rap expression. Suave House, an independent Houston rap label, released hugely successful albums from 8Ball & MJG, and LaFace, a label backed by Arista, set up shop

Big Boi and Andre 3000 (left to right) of OutKast embrace their Atlanta, Georgia, roots, using Southern slang in their lyrics.

in Atlanta and signed OutKast and the Atlanta rap group Goodie Mob.

Despite the achievement of this wave of Southern artists, rappers not located in New York or Los Angeles still had a hard time getting people to take their music seriously. Chingy, a party rhymer from St. Louis, Missouri, best known for his 2003 hits "Right Thurr" and "Holidae In," explains how difficult it was for rappers from smaller cities to break through:

> The challenge of that is that somebody in New York, they have big opportunities. They're around the stuff. We're not around it, so we're struggling four times as hard as them, for real. We've got to wait till somebody comes to the city or we've got to leave out the city to try to go and find people to get them to listen to our music. We don't have big record companies and all that. We don't have none of that, so we've got to really put a gang of effort to try to make it, go out of state and just grind, grind, grind. People from New York, Miami, the West Coast or whatever, they've got it right there with them. It's not that hard. If I was staying in New York or LA, I probably would have made it because I'd have been grinding so tough that you probably couldn't have helped but seen me.[36]

Rappers Create Their Own Opportunities

Their lack of connections to the music industry did not prevent rappers from the South and Midwest from turning advances in recording technology to their advantage. Previously, few artists were able to use studios because they could not afford to buy and store the equipment necessary to record music. Recording equipment was typically large and heavy and required at least two large rooms in order to operate. But as smaller recording equipment became available and personal computers became capable of recording and storing music, making professional-sounding music outside a studio became possible for a whole new generation of artists.

These rappers, eager to get their music heard, skipped the steps of recording an album and shopping a demo to a record company. Instead, they simply made their own albums and released them themselves through their own small record companies, which were typically run out of their homes. Sometimes, after creating a name for themselves by selling their albums in the streets and to select record stores, these small record companies were able to land a deal with a regional distributor.

Eminem Makes a "Shady" Hit

In the mid- and late 1990s, rappers from cities in the South and Midwest became respected national rap stars for the first time. Detroit rapper Eminem was the biggest of these artists. Backed by production from former N.W.A member Dr. Dre, Eminem made controversial antigay statements and recorded a number of songs that seemed to endorse violence, similar to what N.W.A had done nearly a decade before him. In the book Angry Blonde, *Eminem reflects on the making of his smash single "The Real Slim Shady":*

I was tellin' the bass player and keyboard player to play something till I liked it. So they kept [messing] around . . . till Tommy (one of Dre's keyboard players) played the first few notes of "The Real Slim Shady" and I jumped up and said, "What was that?" I then asked him to do something different with it. Make it go up, then down. He did a couple of different things with it until I was like "Right there." I then ran and got Dre to come listen to it. They added drums. Now, this all happened on a Friday. We had a meeting on Saturday with the label and they asked, "Well, did you come up with anything?" I played them "The Way I Am" and they said, "It's a great song. It's just not the first song." Originally, they were talkin' about "Criminal" being the single, but I told them to let me take this [beat] ("The Real Slim Shady" instrumental) over the week-

end and I'd have the rhyme written by Monday. Then we'd see if it worked. If it didn't, then [forget] it. Right around this time was when Will Smith was dissin' gangsta rap and Christina Aguilera was talkin' [trash] about me on MTV, putting me on blast about being married during a time when I wasn't ready for the public to know that about me yet. So I waited just long enough to get new subject matter to get into. Now I had something to talk about. I came in on Monday, recorded it, and was done. . . . That situation made me value the saying "Things happen for a reason" a bit more.

Eminem. *Angry Blonde*. New York: It Books, 2002, pp. 106–107.

Detroit rapper Eminem, seen here in 2010, is one of the biggest stars that came out of the Midwest and South scene of the 1990s.

The larger distribution ensured that the albums of Southern artists were available in more than just their own cities. Rap journalist Matt Sonzala explains:

This breakthrough happened because the Southern artists had to work harder to get noticed than artists in New York or Los Angeles. While the artists on the East and West coast are surrounded by media outlets and other industry aids, the artist and labels in the South, long shunned by their Eastern and Western contemporaries, had to get on the road and work their regions on their own. . . . Houston's Rap-A-Lot Records laid the South's foundation with the Geto Boys and became the backbone of the emerging Southern scene in the early and mid-90s.[37]

Many Southern rappers created such a presence in their own region that the major labels signed them to recording contracts. Says prominent Mississippi rapper David Banner,

If you look at the South, most of us didn't come from demos or having one hot verse on the mix CD. Me, Lil Jon, T.I., Ludacris—we all put out independent albums. We'd all sold hundreds of thousands of records before we got signed [to major labels]. I had more spins than 85 percent of the people that was in the urban department of Universal before I got signed to Universal. So I think that people should respect us as artists and as businessmen.[38]

Master P Hits the Clubs

One of the best of the rappers and businessmen was Master P. Born in New Orleans, the rapper relocated to Richmond, California, about 20 miles (32km) north of San Francisco, and opened a record store, No Limit Records. Master P paid attention to what kind of rap his customers were buying and in the early 1990s decided to launch his own career as a rapper on his own No Limit Records label. Master P noticed that rap fans still wanted to hear hard-hitting gangsta rap, even though the major record companies were moving away from it because of the violence associated with the genre after the deaths of 2Pac and the Notorious B.I.G.

After tirelessly promoting himself and No Limit in the Bay Area and such Southern states as Louisiana and Texas, Master P and other No Limit artists, including Mystikal and Silkk the Shocker, became a force in independent rap music. Rather than make harsh, mid-tempo music like many gangsta rappers before them, they rapped over up-tempo beats that were faster and easier to dance to. Other acts, especially the popular Memphis rap acts 8Ball & MJG and Three 6 Mafia, also made this style of up-tempo gangsta rap and sold millions of albums in the late 1990s.

Atlanta Gets Crunk

The progression of gangster rap into music that could be danced to gained the most momentum in Atlanta. Artists there developed a type of music called crunk, a fiery style typified by aggressive production and choruses chanted like cheers at a pep rally or sporting event.

Atlanta-based Lil Jon & the East Side Boyz are the premier crunk artists.

Atlanta-based Lil Jon & the East Side Boyz are the premier crunk artists. The trio emerged in 1996 with its first album, the independently released *Who U With, Get Crunk:*

The West Coast Fades

After ruling rap in the late 1980s and the early and mid-1990s, the West Coast quickly faded from hip-hop prominence as Southern rappers started dominating in the late 1990s. In this October 2004 interview, Oakland, California, rapper Yukmouth, of the platinum rap duo the Luniz, gives his opinions on why West Coast rap is no longer on top of the rap industry:

I think it's mainly because of the gangbanging. I respect gangbang; it's real serious. But the Bay is unified. We don't gangbang. I can always call E-40, Too $hort, any of them and we're going to do the song. But compared to LA, I can't call Dr. Dre, Snoop, none of them. A lot of LA rappers can't call them, either. It's a difference out here and that's because of the gangbanging that people can't come together because too many family, rela-tives and friends done died over it. People can't let go. But for us to get to the next level, we're going to have to let that go. Put it to the side. Let's squash all that beef and get some money together. That's how the West is going to win. It ain't going to be one artist, one producer that makes beats. It's going to be a unity thing. When 2Pac was alive, we were proud to be from the West Coast 'cause Pac had it unified. Pac had E-40, Too $hort, Dru Down, Daz, Kurupt, Richie Rich, C-Bo, Rappin' 4-Tay. He had New York rappers on his music, too. That's why Pac did it so tight. He unified the West and that's why his *All Eyez on Me* album is Diamond [has sold more than 10 million copies]. You've got to unify to make a statement.

Yukmouth, interview with the author, October 2004.

Da Album. In a 2002 interview Lil Jon explains why Atlanta became so popular for the crunk style of rap:

Atlanta's such a big melting pot. You've got so many different people from so many different areas here. You've got so many different artists that come here just to go to the studio and work. You've got so many big events that happen here. The records that come out of here are exposed to a lot of people that just come in town for the weekend for this or that. That helps to spread the records out. Atlanta artists, we make records straight for the clubs. If your record ain't hitting in the club, then these [people] ain't gonna buy your [music]. You got [artists] that got hot club records that aren't even on the radio that's selling a lot of records in Atlanta. Eventually, those records translate to the radio, but that's the main thing about the Atlanta music scene: We make records for the clubs that will get the clubs cracking. If it ain't getting the clubs cracking, then they ain't buying it. That's how we look at putting the records together.[39]

Cash Money Evolves

While crunk was shaped by the sound Lil Jon created, rap's next movement was defined not by a sonic style, but by the artists themselves. Lil Jon produced songs for artists from New York, Los Angeles, and the South and brought his sound to artists from different regions, but in its initial run in the 1990s, New Orleans–based Cash Money Records released albums full of bouncy beats produced by New Orleans' Mannie Fresh and featuring the gangster-heavy and street-centered rhymes of local rappers B.G., Juvenile, and Lil Wayne and the Big Tymers, among others. For Lil Jon, it was about being a great producer regardless of the artist. For Cash Money, it was about being a successful New Orleans–based label with artists from New Orleans who helped popularize New Orleans slang in lyrics and the city's bouncy music through Mannie Fresh's production.

But by 2006 the departure of B.G., Juvenile, and Mannie Fresh put the future of the label in question. That year, Lil Wayne was given an executive role in the company and through a seemingly endless string of mixtapes, guest appearances, and albums during the next few years, made the rechristened Young Money Cash Money Billionaires Records one of rap's hottest properties. Lil Wayne also showed a keen ear for talent, signing Toronto, Canada, rapper-singer Drake and female New York rapper Nicki Minaj to the imprint.

Although it was groundbreaking for a Southern rapper to endorse and release material by artists from other countries, let alone New York, Nicki Minaj explains that she did not believe that signing with a Southern artist would hurt her career:

> I never worried about that a day in my life. If anything, I just saw Wayne as someone that I looked up to. It didn't matter where he came from. It's weird. With Wayne, I don't consider him a Down South artist. I don't see him like that. He's one of those people that kind of just transcends all that. The New York guys, they knew who I was. They could have reached out, so it never bothered me that I would be coming out with someone that was technically from the South. It made it to me even a more special dynamic because it was unexpected. He probably saw a million female rappers from New Orleans and from all over the world, and he chose me.[40]

As an executive at Young Money Cash Money Billionaires Records, Lil Wayne helped the company become one of the most successful in hip-hop.

DJs Make a Comeback

Thanks in large part to the success of Southern rap acts in the emerging club scene and the increasing presence of rap music on radio stations, DJs again became major hip-hop figures in the mid-1990s. Therefore, even as rap became more and more prominent and graffiti artists and B-boys were increasingly marginalized by mainstream society, DJs were able to develop healthy followings.

To the bigger rap movement, the DJ's main purpose was to support the rapper, if a DJ was used at all. But a number of other developments allowed DJs to become significant fixtures in the rap scene themselves. A crop of DJs who created mixtapes, released their own albums, toured and performed with rock-and-roll groups, and appeared on television programs became increasingly popular.

Mixtape Culture Explodes

Excitement and energy describe the mixtape culture that became a formidable force in the rap industry. Mixtapes were around long before "Rapper's Delight" was released. In the early and mid-1970s, DJs assembled the most popular R&B, soul, funk, and disco songs and put them on a cassette tape. These were called mixtapes because the songs from various artists were mixed together. The DJs then sold the tapes at their performances and in the streets to fans, thereby earning money and recognition.

Once rap songs became popular in the early 1980s, DJs included rap songs on their mixtapes. Later in the 1980s, DJs such as Kid Capri and Ron G realized that they could

B-boys Bounce Back

Once rap became the prominent component of hip-hop in the late 1980s, B-boying was relegated to the background. B-boys enjoyed a boost in popularity in 2008 when record producer and *American Idol* judge Randy Jackson launched *Randy Jackson Presents America's Best Dance Crew*. The MTV program featured groups of B-boys and B-girls performing against each other in an elimination tournament for a $100,000 prize.

In an article titled "'America's Best Dance Crew' Season 6: Superstars and a Super New Judge," published on the website buddytv.com, John Kubicek explains the appeal of the show:

> The show always brings innovative, hip-hop dance crews together, which makes for some of the most entertaining television. It's basically like a full hour of the Tabitha and Napoleon routines from *So You Think You Can Dance*, without any of that boring Viennese Waltz stuff in between.

John Kubicek. "'America's Best Dance Crew' Season 6: Superstars and a Super New Judge." Buddytv.com, April 7, 2011. www.buddytv.com/articles/americas-best-dance-crew/americas-best-dance-crew-seaso-39906.aspx.

also make mixtapes solely of rap songs and that those mixtapes were even more popular among their customers.

In the 1990s mixtapes, especially those in New York, began to feature unreleased music from artists. Individual DJs tried to forge relationships with star rappers in the hopes that the rappers would give them a copy of new songs first. This arrangement gave such DJs as Funkmaster Flex and DJ Clue? a reputation for having the newest music and made them celebrities in their own right.

Even though rappers enjoyed the exposure and attention their songs garnered from mixtapes, many DJs earned the ire of record companies because their mixtapes featured music that the companies did not authorize for release. DJs therefore labeled many mixtapes "for promotional use only" and did not technically offer them for sale. That way, the record companies could not sue the DJs because they could claim they were not selling the mixtapes.

DJs Release Major Albums

As DJs regained their status throughout the 1990s, a number of high-profile DJs graduated from releasing their own self-funded and self-distributed mixtapes to signing deals with major record companies to release albums nationally. The albums from DJs came in a variety of formats.

Pioneering mixtape DJ Kid Capri released *The Tape* in the early 1990s. Although the album features the popular DJ rapping, it failed to garner much interest. It took several years for a mixtape DJ to get another chance to put an album out on a national level. Then popular club and radio DJ Funkmaster Flex broke through in the mid-1990s with *The Mix Tape* series of albums, which were like traditional mixtapes. The albums contain a number of classic rap songs as well as songs exclusive to the album.

DJ Clue?'s *The Professional* album, which arrived in 1998, is in the format of his popular mixtapes. It features all original material from the hottest rappers and R&B artists of the moment, including DMX and Jay-Z.

Another type of album put out by DJs featured the DJs scratching over their own self-produced beats. Released by such DJs as the X-ecutioners, these albums were showcases for the mixing, scratching, and production skills of the DJ, unlike the majority of mixtapes and the albums put out by DJ Clue? and DJ Kayslay, among others, which featured popular rappers rather than the DJs' own turntable dexterity.

50 Cent Changes the Mixtape Landscape

Mixtapes and mixtape DJs remained a largely New York phenomenon until about 2002, when 50 Cent changed the way mixtapes were made. 50 Cent was released from his recording contract with major label Columbia Records when he was shot and almost killed in 2000. After recovering, 50 Cent resumed making music. Unable to get a new recording contract, 50 Cent took instrumental versions of popular songs and made his own covers of them. He then compiled the cuts with his DJ Whoo Kid onto mixtapes and released them to the underground mixtape scene in New York.

50 Cent's success with mixtapes helped elevate the standing of DJs in hip-hop.

The strategy paid off for 50 Cent, who featured his rhyme crew, the G Unit, on many of his mixtape releases. With his name building in New York and radio stations playing his mixtape songs on the radio, something that had rarely happened before, several record companies started pursuing the rapper. In 2002 50 Cent signed to Dr. Dre's Aftermath Entertainment and Eminem's Shady Records. After selling more than 10 million copies of his own albums, 50 Cent still releases mixtapes, although less frequently than he did before signing with Dr. Dre and Eminem.

The explosion of the mixtape culture, thanks in large part to the success of 50 Cent, increased the standing of DJs in the hip-hop world. In 2005 DJs such as Green Lantern and DJ Drama released mixtapes (today released either on CD or digitally online) that earned as much attention as some albums. In fact, the mixtape DJs are so popular and have such big followings that many rappers give their new songs to mixtape DJs before they give them to anyone else—including their record label.

Rock Groups and Television Embrace DJs

As the mixtape culture developed in the late 1990s and more DJs secured major record deals, DJs became more prominent through their work independent of rappers rather than with them. Even though rappers typically distanced themselves from DJs, the DJs got a boost from a seemingly unlikely source: rock groups. Rock acts that incorporated some rapping into their work, such as Limp Bizkit and Kid Rock, featured DJs during their live performances. Around the same time, television shows such as *The Chris Rock Show* and *Chappelle's Show* featured DJs hired to segue the program into and out of commercial breaks.

After several years in which their value diminished, DJs are again a visible and crucial portion of the hip-hop landscape. With their high visibility, several DJs also have become international draws, a key component of hip-hop's global explosion.

CHAPTER 7

Hip-Hop:
A Global Force

As hip-hop developed in the mid-1970s, DJs were the cornerstone of the culture. So when DJ and hip-hop pioneer Afrika Bambaataa organized the first European hip-hop tour in 1982, he established himself—and, by default, DJs in general—as the culture's unofficial ambassador around the world. The Bambaataa tour included DJs, B-boys, rappers, and graffiti artists. By introducing Europe to all aspects of hip-hop culture, the tour allowed each segment of the culture to evolve outside the United States.

So, even though rap has been the most recognized and popular component of hip-hop culture since it exploded in the late 1980s, the other components have enjoyed sustained levels of respect and acclaim throughout the world. Also, as in the United States, where each segment of hip-hop culture grew out of other forms of art, international hip-hop followed a similar path by morphing into new styles and sounds based on the American originals and the business models of American hip-hop businessmen.

English Rappers Score

In England, rap quickly developed its own scene. London rapper Derek B released an album in 1988 on Profile

Records, also home to Run-D.M.C. Even though he did not become a major rap force in America, he nonetheless helped establish the London rap scene, because his album encouraged other aspiring British rappers to record their own material and develop their own style of rap.

Starting in the early 1990s, trip-hop, an English form of hip-hop typified by a mixture of break beats and down-tempo electronic music that was popularized by artists like Massive Attack and Tricky, began to catch on in Europe and eventually the rest of the world. The music was especially popular in dance clubs, and its deep, hypnotic grooves were said to be enjoyed more thoroughly if a person was on a drug-induced "trip"—hence the name trip-hop.

Overseas Rappers Fail to Connect

Although there are vibrant rap scenes throughout the world, foreign artists have had a difficult time generating commercial success in the United States. Several rappers from England, including the Streets, Ms. Dynamite, Dizzee Rascal, and Lady Sovereign, enjoyed extensive coverage in the American media, but none became major rap stars in America. The reggaeton subgenre also enjoyed a heavy promotional push in the mid-2000s, but within a few years, its success had stalled and it quickly faded.

One foreign artist who enjoyed noteworthy success in the United States is English rapper-singer M.I.A. Her 2007 single "Paper Planes" sold 3 million digital copies, according to the Recording Industry Association of America, which tracks music sales. The song's commercial success— and M.I.A.'s status in the United States music scene—was bolstered when rapper T.I. sampled "Paper Planes" in his song "Swagga Like Us," a popular selection from his 2008 album *Paper Trail* that also featured Kanye West, Jay-Z, and Lil Wayne.

A segment of trip-hop soon evolved into garage, a style of English hip-hop with faster and heavier drum patterns. This intense style garnered international acclaim thanks to conversational white rapper the Streets, female rapper and R&B singer Ms. Dynamite, and hard-core rapper Dizzee Rascal. All three artists, each with a distinctive sound, style, and image, enjoyed critical acclaim in such high-profile American music magazines as *Rolling Stone* and *Entertainment Weekly*. In fact, in its January 16, 2004, issue, *Entertainment Weekly* gave Dizzee Rascal's *Boy in da Corner* album the lead review, a distinction reserved for an album of particular interest or merit.

MC Solaar Introduces French Rap

Three years after Derek B brought British rap international attention, French-based rapper MC Solaar earned an international following because of his nimble raps and the jazz-inspired music over which he rapped. His first album,

MC Solaar performs at Seyne-Sur-Mer, France, in 1995. He was an early producer of rap in a language other than English.

1991's *Qui Seme le Vent Recolte le Tempo* (*He Who Sows the Wind Gathers the Tempo*), was an early example of quality rap performed in a language other than English. As writer Don Snowden explains in his AllMusic review of the album:

> The debut disc from MC Solaar is a clear signal that quality hip-hop can exist outside the U.S. and the English language barriers. Most of his lyrics read as "I'm the man" MC boasts and shout-outs to the Paris hip-hop crew, but the French rapper has superb flow and a masterful producer in Jimmy Jay, an absolute natural when it comes to creating sonic pastiches/collages to fit the lyrics. It's French hip-hop and therefore a softer, gentler sound with the music more on the acid jazz tip to match the rhythm and flavor of Solaar's native tongue. . . . It's an impressive debut and important historically—by pairing a rapper and producer in perfect sync with one another, it gave early French hip-hop a sound and tone of its own from the beginning.[41]

Reggaeton Strikes a Chord

As French rap evolved, people in other countries began creating their own styles of rap, too. Reggaeton, from Puerto Rico, is a popular, typically energetic hybrid of rap and reggae, the indigenous music of Jamaica popularized by the laid-back "roots" style of Bob Marley and the more aggressive, rap-influenced dance-hall style of Buju Banton, Sean Paul, and others. Hip-hop and reggaeton, which is typically performed in Spanish, share many similarities. Reggaeton is, in the words of popular artist Tego Calderon, "the new way the youth here in [Puerto Rico] express themselves; mainly it was a form of expression among the poor. It started out the same way as hip-hop did. Initially, it was totally underground. In a 10-year span people got used to listening to our music, and the music earned a space in radio shows."[42] Like hip-hop acts, reggaeton artists have a number of different musical styles. Calderon incorporates political messages into his material, while Daddy Yankee and Pitbull have scored international hits with their infectious dance music.

The Japanese Hip-Hop Scene

As reggaeton gains popularity throughout the world, Japan remains prominent on the world hip-hop scene. As in the 1970s in the Bronx, New York, each segment of hip-hop culture is celebrated there with virtually equal attention. The Japanese affinity for B-boys is so strong that there is a Japanese Rock Steady Crew, as well as a number of other B-boy crews, including ZOO.

Two of Japan's first and most recognized hip-hop artists are DJ Krush and DJ Honda. Best known for his production prowess, DJ Krush specializes in deep, meditative, and moody beats that have hip-hop–inspired percussion and also include traditional Japanese music. DJ Honda, on the other hand, is known for his minimalist, drum-heavy production that sounds similar to that of New York rap producers of the mid-1990s.

Even though many Japanese rappers and fans do not understand or speak English, that has not stopped hip-hop from being accepted and practiced in their country. As writer Geo Hagan notes, "The Hip Hop movement is itself a revolution that started in the streets and has grown to be the most influential cultural force the world over. There are kids in Japan that don't understand a word of English, but can still recite a Jay-Z album from beginning to end."[43]

Jay-Z Helps Punjabi MC

In addition to having millions of fans in the United States and Japan, Jay-Z helped catapult Punjabi MC to stardom in 2003 when he appeared on the remix of Punjabi MC's "Beware of the Boys." The word *Punjabi* refers to a member of the majority people of Punjab in northwestern India, and Punjabi MC, who lives in England, took his stage name as a nod to his Indian heritage.

Jay-Z's appearance on the song made it a hit in the United States, but more importantly, "Beware of the Boys" introduced a hip-hop take on bhangra, a Punjabi dance music traditionally performed during harvest festivals and weddings, characterized by the beating of a large two-headed drum. The song, as well as the work of American producer

Punjabi MC, seen here at the 2003 MTV Europe Music Awards, introduced a hip-hop take on Indian bhangra dance music.

Timbaland and others, helped popularize bhangra with rap fans around the world. In his review of *Beware*, the album on which "Beware of the Boys" appears, writer Dan LeRoy explains the album's international significance: "As an authentic antidote to hip-hop's superficial Indian infatuation, Beware is most welcome; what it augurs [predicts] for future musical meetings between East and West makes it most important as well."[44]

Jay-Z, Master of All Trades

Jay-Z's appearance on the remix to Punjabi MC's "Beware of the Boys" in 2003 increased the Brooklynite's international status. He released his first album, *Reasonable Doubt*, in 1996, but it was not until two years and two albums later that this rapper became a rap power broker. Released in 1998, *Vol. 2 . . . Hard Knock Life* made Jay-Z into one of rap's elite and gave him the platform to flex his entrepreneurial muscle. In January 2005 Jay-Z took over as president and CEO of Roc-A-Fella Records and Def Jam Recordings, the latter being the most recognized and respected rap label in the world. Writer Jason Birchmeier details the first portion of Jay-Z's music career on www .allmusic.com:

> Embodying the rags-to-riches rap dream, Jay-Z pulled himself up by his bootstraps as a youth to eventually become the reigning rapper

of New York City and, in turn, a major-label executive following his short-lived retirement from music-making. In the wake of his 1996 debut, *Reasonable Doubt*, Jay-Z's albums sold millions upon millions with each release, and his endless parade of hits made him omnipresent on urban radio and video television. He retained a strongly devoted fan base and challenged whatever rivals attempted to oust him from atop the rap game; sparring most memorably with Nas. Jay-Z and his Roc-a-Fella associates greatly influenced the industry and established many of the trends that pervaded during the late '90s and early 2000s. He consistently worked with the hottest producers of the day (. . . DJ Premier, Teddy Riley, Track Masters, Erick Sermon, Timbaland, Swizz Beatz),

Worldwide Struggle

Fans around the world hold American rappers such as Jay-Z in high regard, but they often feel a special connection with rappers from their own countries, who rap in the native language about topics relevant to their homeland. Rappers around the world have taken their American predecessors' cue by using their raps to discuss political issues and express their outrage at social injustices. In Mexico, for example, rappers discuss drugs, violence, and Mexican Indian pride, while in Brazil rappers discuss life in the na-

and if they weren't hot at the time, they likely would be afterward (. . . Kanye West, Just Blaze, 9th Wonder). He similarly collaborated with the hottest rappers in the industry, everyone from East Coast contemporaries like the Notorious B.I.G. . . . and DMX . . . to the best rappers from the South (Ludacris, Missy Elliott) and the West Coast (Snoop Dogg, Too Short).

In July 2005 Jay-Z announced the launch of Roc La Familia, a Def Jam subsidiary that would release albums from reggae, reggaeton, calypso, tribal, and West Indian artists. Since then Jay-Z has founded the Roc Nation record label, released a *New York Times* best-selling first book, purchased a minority share in the professional basketball team the New Jersey Nets, and married R&B singer Beyoncé.

Jason Birchmeier. "Jay-Z." AllMusic. www.allmusic .com/artist/jay-z-p195154.

Jay-Z is a leading power broker in hip-hop and pop music.

tion's ghettos, known as favelas. In the African country of Ghana, rappers discuss how AIDS is ravaging the country, while in Israel rappers offer their opinions regarding the Israeli-Palestinian conflict.

While the work of these rappers resonates most strongly with people in their own countries, it has increasingly been gaining notice in other parts of the world. *The Source*, the most recognized American rap magazine, has Latino and French editions that discuss matters of political significance, and also features an annual international section in its domestic edition that highlights the work of hip-hop practitioners around the world. Also, thanks in part to the Internet, which allows songs to be transferred electronically, it is as easy for a rap fan in Turkey to listen to a protest song by an Israeli rapper as it is for a Kenyan enthusiast to hear the work of a Brazilian rap artist famous for writing political songs.

China Controls Rap

Even though rap retains its rebellious edge throughout much of the world, in China many rappers create music the government endorses and even promotes. In an article titled "You Can't Get a Bad Rap Here," *Los Angeles Times* staff writer Ralph Frammolino explains that Chinese rappers release tame music that embraces government policy:

> Instead of often obscene and violent tales from the inner city, . . . leading rappers here are taking to the stage with lyrics that glorify national pride, celebrate tourist attractions and preach against the dangers of adolescent impulsiveness. One group is so proud of its songs that it has affixed a sticker to its debut album asking fans to share it with their parents. State-controlled television features public service announcements in rap about caring for the environment and respecting elders, leading one academic to suggest that hip-hop has become the unofficial music of the Communist government.[45]

In fact, Frammolino notes that the writings of former Chinese ruler Mao Zedong inspired a Chinese rap album that was released in 2003 in conjunction with his 110th birthday.

But not all Chinese hip-hop supporters find the Chinese government's involvement with the work of rap artists appealing. As Beijing-area disc jockey Chen "MC Allan" Shen explains, Chinese rappers "can't curse, they basically have to say life is great, life is beautiful, nothing's wrong. . . . It's not hip-hop."[46]

Hip-Hop as Global Business

What hip-hop is and is not continues to be defined as it spreads throughout the world. The globalization of business and the increased ease of international travel have helped each element of hip-hop culture become a significant tool for selling products internationally for a variety of corporations. Today rap albums are among the best-selling albums around the world. Furthermore, rappers are now viewed as reputable spokespeople and are paid to promote such products as soft drinks and deodorant in advertising campaigns used by major corporations in the United States and Europe.

A prime example of hip-hop's international commercial viability is the presence rappers have in the tennis shoe market. Shoe companies, which realized the importance of embracing hip-hop in the 1980s with Run-D.M.C. and in the 1990s with Master P, fully incorporated hip-hop culture in the new millennium. By the end of 2003 Jay-Z had his own "The S. Carter" shoe through Reebok, 50 Cent had his own "The G Unit" shoe through Reebok, and Nelly teamed with Nike to release a limited-edition "Air Derrty" shoe.

Headphones: Music to Businessmen's Ears

Dr. Dre is widely regarded as the best rap producer of all time. The California-based artist's work with N.W.A, Snoop Dogg, Eminem, and 50 Cent helped propel and define the genre in the 1980s, 1990s, and 2000s. One complaint rap enthusiasts have with Dr. Dre, though, is his lack of music output throughout the 2000s. In 2008 Dre revealed at least one reason why he had been keeping a low musical profile. He had been developing a new product, one that required he shift some of his focus away from making music. The producer had teamed with record executive Jimmy Iovine to launch Beats by Dre, a line of high-end headphones. The headphones quickly became a status symbol among music aficionados and celebrities. In 2011 a majority stake in Beats by Dre was sold for a reported $300 million to mobile-phone company HTC, a global business with extensive operations in the United States, as well as Asia and Europe.

The Swedish company WeSC partnered in 2011 with rapper-producer RZA to launch a line of headphones, the Chambers by RZA. Ludacris also has his own headphones, a testament to the ever-expanding ways rappers attempt to expand their business throughout the globe.

These deals, promoted around the world, marked the first time that nonathletes were used to endorse athletic shoes.

As rap's influence continues to grow, the other segments of hip-hop culture have grown, too. Graffiti, for instance, regained its commercial acceptance in the 1990s and has again become a bankable practice. Journalist Laura Checkoway explains, "By 2000, art galleries, once shunned by those who conceived of graffiti as public art, were selling canvases with five-figure price tags, and high-end designers hit the runways with graf-inspired creations."[47]

Rap group Native Deen—seen here performing at the 2011 Ramadan Festival in Indonesia—fuses African American and Islamic cultures to convey its message.

Hip-Hop as International Bridge

In addition to being a prime source of commerce throughout the world, hip-hop has also been used as an international unification tool. For instance, in 2002 a rap song was promoted to celebrate the end of Ramadan, a monthlong Muslim holiday with daily fasting. As writer Anwar Iqbal explains,

This year the end of Ramadan in New York will be celebrated with a hip-hop song called "Muslim." An

African-American group called Native Deen will perform this and other songs in front of an expected audience of 1,000. . . . The Washington-based group borrows its name from an Arabic word "deen," meaning faith, and fuses African-American and Islamic cultures to convey its message: pray five times a day, do not smoke or drink and be proud of Islam."[48]

CHAPTER 8

The New Rap Landscape

As hip-hop culture becomes more interwoven into larger American society, it enjoys steady success as a commodity. Once shunned by corporate America, rappers, graffiti artists, DJs, and B-boys hawk a range of products more diverse than ever, from computers to cars to clothes and soft drinks. The genre is more pervasive than ever and its once regional borders have fallen.

But as hip-hop's reach expands throughout the business world, sales of albums throughout the music industry are down significantly, including those of rappers. At least some of the sales decline is due to the rampant illegal downloading and file sharing of music, something the record industry did not have to contend with until the 2000s. Furthermore, several prominent record store chains, including Tower Records and Virgin Megastore, closed during the 2000s, providing fewer locations for consumers to purchase music legally. All of this news was compounded by the economic recession that hit the United States in 2007, leaving many Americans with less disposable income.

Sales Shrink

In 2004 total album sales in the United States were 666.7 million. The best-selling album of that year, Usher's

Confessions, sold 8 million copies thanks in large part to the single "Yeah!" which was produced by Lil Jon and featured Ludacris. In 2010 326.2 million albums were sold, which was a 12.7 percent decrease from 2009 and is less than half the number of albums sold in 2004.

While those numbers show that the record industry is suffering because of free music on the Internet and the closure of hundreds of record stores among other factors, rap produced some of the most positive sales news in 2010. The best-selling album of 2010 was Eminem's *Recovery*, which sold more than 3.4 million copies. Furthermore, in 2010 two of the three best-selling songs in digital formats featured rappers: Katy Perry's "California Gurls" featured Snoop Dogg and sold 4.4 million copies, while Eminem's

Emergence of White Rappers

During the first few decades of rap's existence, the overwhelming majority of rap artists were black. The few white rappers who emerged in the 1980s and early 1990s faced skepticism about their dedication to hip-hop culture and their credibility from some rap fans. Despite the added scrutiny from the rap community and others, white rap acts the Beastie Boys and Eminem became among the genre's best-selling artists of all time.

As Eminem exploded in popularity in the late 1990s by making his race a significant part of his subject matter, white rappers such as Dilated People's Evidence and Atmosphere's Slug created successful careers for themselves without making their race an issue in their music.

By 2011 white rappers such as Yelawolf, Mac Miller, Machine Gun Kelly, and Kreayshawn were being presented as rappers, not just white rappers. Their race was certainly a part of their appeal to some fans, but for the first time in rap's thirty-plus-year history, a generation of white rappers was being primarily evaluated by the majority of listeners based on the quality of their music, not their race.

"Love The Way You Lie" featuring Rihanna sold 4.2 million copies. By comparison, the best-selling rap digital track of 2004, the Black Eyed Peas' "Let's Get It Started," sold 328,000 copies.

But Eminem's robust sales pale in comparison to his previous sales figures. The Detroit rapper's 2002 album, *The Eminem Show*, for instance, sold 7.6 million copies. That is more than double the amount *Recovery* sold in 2010. As writer David Goldman explains in his "Music's Lost Decade: Sales Cut in Half" article from money.cnn.com:

> At the end of [2010], the music business was worth half of what it was ten years ago and the decline doesn't look like it will be slowing anytime soon. Total revenue from U.S. music sales and licensing plunged to $6.3 billion in 2009, according to Forrester Research. In 1999, that revenue figure topped $14.6 billion. Although the Recording Industry Association of America will report its official figures in the early spring, the trend has been very clear: RIAA has reported declining revenue in nine of the past 10 years, with album sales falling an average of 8% each year. Last decade was the first ever in which sales were lower going out than coming in.[49]

Sales figures alone do not tell the entire story, however. On the Internet-based video service YouTube.com, the official version of Eminem's "Love The Way You Lie" video has more than 410 million views as of December 2010. This suggests that even though consumers are not purchasing music at the same rate that they used to, they are still consuming music at high levels.

Rappers Launch Careers Online

As evidenced by Eminem's views on YouTube.com, music is being consumed on the Internet by millions of people. One rapper who capitalized on the increasing power of the Internet to spread music instantly and without cost was Soulja Boy Tell'em, who now records as Soulja Boy. After recording and releasing his music independently on the Internet for nearly two years, Soulja Boy recorded and posted the song "Crank That (Soulja Boy)" on the Web in

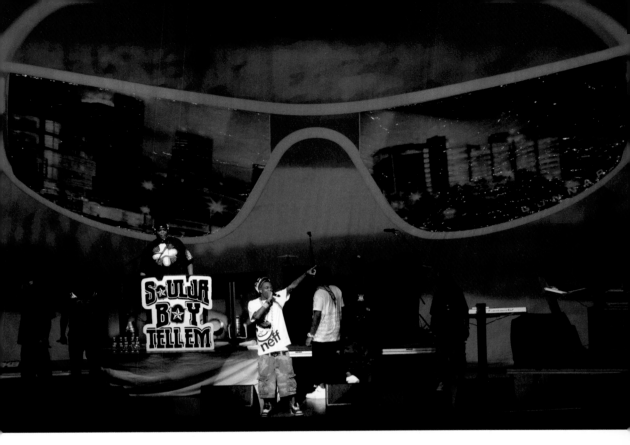

early 2007. Within a few months, the song became a sensation thanks to its low-budget video, which features Soulja Boy showcasing the "Crank That" dance, a simple yet catchy dance where people bounce from side to side while leaning and moving their hands as though they are cranking the throttle on a motorcycle.

Prior to this time, aspiring artists would record material and offer it to record companies, established music producers, or veteran artists. These artists hoped that their music would appeal to one of the established music industry insiders, who would then sign them to a recording contract. Soulja Boy, on the other hand, skipped all intermediaries by using the biggest distribution outlet in the world to promote his music. By releasing his music independently on the Internet, Soulja Boy bypassed the traditional way artists had often broken into the music industry.

Veteran rap producer Mr. ColliPark, who had worked with Ying Yang Twins, David Banner, and others, signed the

Soulja Boy Tell'em found success by uploading his music independently to the Internet.

Old Rapper, New Label

For many up-and-coming recording artists, getting re-leased from their recording contract before they put out their first album would signal the end of their careers. In the new rap landscape, the Internet, mixtapes, and social media enable rappers to create, sustain, or reestablish a buzz with fans without the backing of a major record label. Wiz Khalifa and Freddie Gibbs, for instance, are among a new generation of rappers who turned their newfound contractual freedom into opportunity.

Upon his release from Warner Bros. Records in 2009, Wiz Khalifa became prolific. In fewer than two years he released a bevy of mixtapes, an independent album, and collaborated with other artists on dozens of songs. Wiz was rewarded in 2010 with a recording contract with Atlantic Records and his single "Black And Yellow" reached the number-one spot on Billboard's Hot 100 chart in February 2011.

In a February 2011 interview, Wiz Khalifa explained the lessons he learned when he was dropped from Warner Bros. Records: "I basically just learned to work for myself and keep everything internal, stick with the people you've been grinding with, just to put on the home team. Stick with that and be able to present that to a label, rather than letting them determine what your marketing and stuff like that is going to be like."

Wiz Khalifa, phone interview with the author, February 11, 2011.

then sixteen-year-old Soulja Boy to a recording contract. The song "Crank That" became a hit online, was featured on the cable television program *Entourage*, and peaked at number one on the Billboard Hot 100 chart, which tracks the sale of singles. As of 2011 the song had sold more than 3 million mastertones (also known as ringtones).

Given the almost instant success of "Crank That (Soulja Boy)" when Soulja Boy released the song on his own and the tune's continued success once he aligned himself with Mr. ColliPark, Soulja Boy did not go through the typically long process of recording albums' worth of material before landing a recording contract, as is the case with most artists. As Soulja Boy explains on his website:

> I'm not like a child star, where people watched you grow up your entire life. I've only been in the spotlight for a year and a half or so. *Souljaboytellem.com* dropped October 2, 2007, and here we are now. But so much has happened in this past year and a half it seems like it's been a long, long time. People look at me like I'm a marketing genius, and they ask me for advice, but I was just a kid having fun. I can't tell you how to live life. This isn't a scheme or a secret I can uncover for you. It just unfolded with my success.[50]

Soulja Boy's rise marked a new way for artists to gain entrance to the music industry. The Internet leveled the playing field for emerging rap artists by giving independent artists who had limited financial resources to make professional-looking, high-budget videos or tour the country a place to distribute their music, instantly making it accessible to anyone who wanted to listen to it. It also signaled several other shifts in how rap was being consumed and created.

Rap Loses Regionalism

One of these shifts has been in the way listeners discover new artists and songs. In the 1980s and 1990s and the early part of the 2000s, music lovers encountered fresh sounds through rap videos shown on MTV, BET, and other television networks. Another way for listeners to discover new music was through radio stations. But these outlets restricted the listeners' experience by selecting which songs and videos were played and when they were played.

With the Internet, these barriers no longer existed. People could choose which videos they wanted to watch or which songs they wanted to listen to online without having to wait to see if a music video program would play the video on television or listen to a radio station with the hopes of

Nicki Minaj, a Rare Female Rap Star

There have been few female rappers of note throughout rap's history. Early rap stars Salt 'N Pepa were able to sustain success for several years by balancing their sex appeal with catchy pop music, but hypersexual rappers such as Lil' Kim, Foxy Brown, and Trina lost much of their luster among fans and critics once the shock of their explicit lyrics and imagery wore off.

Nicki Minaj is a female rapper who has been able to become a legitimate rap star. The Queens, New York, rapper is a clever lyricist whose affiliation with Lil Wayne and imaginative and ever-changing image have helped fuel her success. She has used her inventive wordplay, playful sexuality, catchy beats, and multiple musical personas to become one of rap's most popular acts. The following is a portion of writer David Jeffries' review of Minaj's debut album, 2010's *Pink Friday*, from www.allmusic.com:

> Feed off the production, the great musical ideas, and Minaj's keen sense of her surroundings, and *Pink Friday* is an outstanding success. It's chock-full of new wave textures and diva attitude, creating the kind of atmosphere where will.i.am stops over while you tell the haters to kill themselves over a "Video Killed the Radio Star" sample ("Check It Out"). More grand moments come when Kanye West and Minaj mack together on

the great, Simple Minds–sampling "Blazin," or when "Your Love" waltzes out of the speakers with a unique brand of hood majesty.

David Jeffries. "Nicki Minaj Pink Friday Review." All Music. www.allmusic.com/album/pink-friday-r2053577/review.

Nicki Minaj, one of rap's biggest stars, performs at the 2010 Hot 97 Summer Jam.

hearing a song. Now, because of the Internet, access was immediate and, as time went on, increasingly vast.

Listeners on the Web could now instantly listen to music beyond just what was popular in their geographic region. For example, a New York rap fan who grew up in the 1990s and enjoyed the music of West Coast artists, such as Ice Cube and Too $hort, most likely would not have been able to hear their material on the radio because the rap music at the time tended to be region-specific. A New York radio station tended to play music from rappers from New York, while a Los Angeles radio station played a heavy dose of music from Los Angeles rappers. In the 2000s, however, that same New York rap fan would be able to go to YouTube, MySpace, and a number of other websites and listen to material from Ice Cube, Too $hort, and virtually any other artist on demand.

In addition to connecting listeners with artists, this shift also allowed like-minded artists to get in touch with each other more easily. When Ice Cube collaborated with the New York–based production team The Bomb Squad to work on his debut album, 1990's *AmeriKKKa's Most Wanted*, it was noteworthy because it marked a collaboration between two established rap entities from different cities.

A decade later, rappers, more than ever before, find it convenient to work with artists from different cities thanks to the ease of connecting with a wider range of artists over the Web. Los Angeles–based rapper Murs, for instance, has released collaborative albums with North Carolina–based producer 9th Wonder and New York–based producer Ski Beatz, as well as rapper Slug, of the Minneapolis, Minnesota–based duo Atmosphere.

Slug, in particular, faced tremendous challenges trying to break into the rap industry in the 1990s because he was one of the first rappers from Minneapolis who tried to make a career in the field. Today, there is a vibrant rap scene there that Slug and Atmosphere helped build. As Slug explains:

We kind of made people take notice of Minneapolis so now if you're fly, if you're dope, if your [music] is good, people aren't just going to laugh at you for being from Minneapolis anymore like they used to. They'll give you a second and if you're dope, it'll click. Whereas back then, just being like, "I'm from Minneapolis," people were like, "Where?" It's near Chicago is what we'd have to say, but it ain't near Chicago. It's seven hours by car from Chicago. But people didn't get it.[51]

Artists from different regions of the United States creating music together has a direct impact on the sound, style, and feel of the songs they create. For instance, Ice Cube is a Los Angeles–based artist whose biggest hits have tended to be funky and laid-back. But when he worked with Atlanta-based producer Lil Jon on the 2006 song "Go To Church," the result sounded much more like the type of sonically aggressive material Lil Jon is famous for than the more mellow sounds typical of Ice Cube. Without collaborating with Lil Jon, an artist from another city, Ice Cube may not have rapped as fast or with as much energy as he did on "Go To Church" because it was not his typical style at that point in his career.

Technology Allows for Other Changes

Rappers working with more and different types of artists is also possible for other reasons. In interviews, rappers regularly mention that they were not in the same studio when they recorded a song with an artist who appears on the track with them. That is able to happen because of the evolution of technology.

Music producers are able to e-mail the file of a song while it is being recorded to another artist or musician anywhere in the world. The artist can then download the song, record their material, and e-mail it back to the producer. The producer can then make the song by adding the elements from the different performers without ever having the artists together in the same studio.

Rapper Game, for instance, received the music for the song that would eventually become "Red Nation" from his 2011 album, *The R.E.D. Album*, while on tour in Germany. The song also features Lil Wayne. Game, the producers Cool & Dre, and Lil Wayne were not in the studio at the same time during the majority of the recording process. As Game explains:

I'm in Germany at the time, in a snowstorm, when I got the beat. Me and one of my best friends, AR, we started writing it right away. I wrote three verses, and by the time I got home, my verses were old and I didn't like them anymore. Once Wayne sent me his version of the hook, I had to rewrite all three of the verses. I rewrote them in like a half an hour.[52]

Rapper Game has taken advantage of new technology that allows him work on an album while touring, as musicians no longer have to be in the same studio to produce a record.

A Hip-Hop World

Hip-hop, which started out as something fun to do in Bronx neighborhoods in the 1970s, has become a billion-dollar business that reaches into virtually every aspect of life. Indeed, thirty years after its inception, hip-hop's influence is almost everywhere. Rap songs are among the most popular on the urban and pop radio stations. Major motion pictures regularly feature rappers in starring roles. International turntable organizations thrive in the United States, Germany, and Japan. Many streets in metropolitan areas around the world have some sort of street art, whether it is illegal graffiti, a commissioned mural, or a painting completed with a hip-hop flair.

As it continues to evolve, hip-hop shows little sign of losing its hold on popular culture around the world. Andre Harrell, the founder of Uptown Records, who helped launch the careers of Diddy, Mary J. Blige, Jodeci, Heavy D & the Boyz, and others, recognizes the universal appeal of hip-hop culture. "Rich, poor, Asian, Hispanic, black, white, they're all part of the hip hop generation," Harrell says. "Hip hop just gives everyone an opportunity. Everybody knows where it comes from, everybody loves it. And it's never going away."[53]

NOTES

Chapter 1: The Roots of Hip-Hop Culture

1. Quoted in Greg Kot. "Bambaataa: 'All music is dance music.'" *Chicago Tribune*, October 12, 2004. www.chicagotribune.com.
2. Kot. "Bambaataa."
3. Quoted in Kot. "Bambaataa."
4. Quoted in Billy Jam. "Creator of the Scratch: Grand Wizard Theodore." Hip Hop Slam, 2001. www.hiphopslam.com.

Chapter 2: Hip-Hop Gains Momentum

5. Quoted in Jenny Eliscu. "The Music Q&A." *Rolling Stone*, September 4, 2003, p. 62.
6. Jayo Felony, in-person interview with the author, Glendale, California, April 26, 2005.
7. Quoted in Kot. "Bambaataa."
8. QD3, in-person interview with the author, Studio City, California, March 23, 2005.
9. Quoted in Kot. "Bambaataa."
10. The Reverend Run with Curtis L. Taylor. *It's Like That*. New York: St. Martin's Press, 2000, p. 30.

Chapter 3: The Golden Era of Rap

11. Quoted in Austin Scaggs. "The Music Q&A." *Rolling Stone*, August 7, 2003, p. 30.
12. Stephen Thomas Erlewine. "Salt-N-Pepa." AllMusic. www.allmusic.com/artist/salt-n-pepa-p92/biography.
13. MC Lyte, in-person interview with the author, Chicago, Illinois, February 6, 2003.
14. Fabolous, phone interview with the author, February 2003.
15. Quoted in Reginald C. Dennis. *The Very Best of Big Daddy Kane* (liner notes). Warner Bros. Records and Rhino Entertainment, 2001.
16. Big Daddy Kane, phone interview with the author, March 2003.
17. Stephen Thomas Erlewine. "Public Enemy." AllMusic. www.allmusic.com/artist/public-enemy-p86.

Chapter 4: Gangsta Rap

18. Schoolly D, phone interview with the author, March 2003.
19. David Mills. "Los Angeles' Gangsters of Rap, Escalating the Attitude." *Washington Post*, May 20, 1990.

20. David Mills. "Rap's Hostile Fringe." *Washington Post*, September 12, 1990, p. G1.
21. J.D. Considine. "Rap Capital Shifts from N.Y. to L.A." *Baltimore Sun*, April 23, 1989, p. 1M.
22. Quoted in John Leland and Linda Buckley. "Number One with a Bullet." *Newsweek*, July 1, 1991.
23. Mills. "Los Angeles' Gangsters of Rap."
24. Richard Harrington. "Rap's Unheard Riot Warning." *Washington Post*, May 27, 1992, p. C7.
25. LL Cool J with Karen Hunter. *I Make My Own Rules*. New York: St. Martin's Press, 1997, p. 190.
26. Mills. "Los Angeles' Gangsters of Rap."
27. Lorraine Ali. "The 90s Era–Smells Like Teen Spirit." *Rolling Stone*, May 15, 1997, p. 97.
28. Quoted in Laura Parker. "Rap Group Acquitted in Florida." *Washington Post*, October 21, 1990, p. A1.
29. Jonathan Yardley. "Art and the Oeuvre of 2 Live Crew." *Washington Post*, October 22, 1990, p. B2.

Chapter 5: Rap Business Explodes

30. Julio G, phone interview with the author, March 15, 2005.
31. Phyllis Pollack, phone interview with the author, March 14, 2005.
32. Tomica Wright, phone interview with the author, March 15, 2005.

33. Layzie Bone, phone interview with the author, March 9, 2005.
34. Young Noble, phone interview with the author, March 18, 2005.

Chapter 6: Rise of the South and of the DJ

35. Quoted in Lang Whitaker. "Double Shots." *XXL*, August 2003, p. 86.
36. Chingy, in-person interview with the author, Los Angeles, California, October 27, 2004.
37. Matt Sonzala. "Rise of the South." *The Official Guide to The Source Awards 2003*, p. 72.
38. Quoted in Hillary Crosley, "Blessed by Lil Scrappy, Produced By Lil Jon, David Banner Gets Certified." MTV.com, May 6, 2005. www.mtv.com/news/articles/1501362/david-banner-gets-certified.jhtml.
39. Lil Jon, phone interview with the author, August 2002.
40. Nicki Minaj, in-person interview with the author, March 21, 2010.

Chapter 7: Hip-Hop: A Global Force

41. Don Snowden. "Qui Seme le Vent Recolte le Tempo." AllMusic. www.allmusic.com/album/r208833.
42. Quoted in Ninoska Marcano M. "Q and A with Tego Calderon." *Baltimore Sun*, November 11, 2004, p. 5T.

43. Geo Hagan. "The Pimping of an Icon." *Rime*, Issue 8, 2003, p. 18.

44. Dan LeRoy. "Beware." AllMusic. www.allmusic.com/album/r649434.

45. Ralph Frammolino. "You Can't Get a Bad Rap Here." *Los Angeles Times*, November 12, 2004. http://articles.latimes.com/2004/nov/12/world/fg-chinarap12.

46. Frammolino. "You Can't Get a Bad Rap Here."

47. Laura Checkoway. "State of the Elements." *Vibe*, September 2003, p. 114.

48. Anwar Iqbal. "Americans Add Hip-Hop to Ramadan." United Press International, November 27, 2002. www.upi.com/view.cfm?StoryID=20021127-025310-5260r.

Chapter 8: The New Rap Landscape

49. David Goldman. "Music's Lost Decade: Sales Cut in Half." money.cnn.com, February 3, 2010. http://money.cnn.com/2010/02/02/news/companies/napster_music_industry.

50. Quoted in "About." Soulja Boy: The DeAndre Way. www.thedeandreway.com/bio.

51. Slug, phone interview with the author, April 7, 2011.

52. Game, in-person interview with the author, Inglewood, California, August, 18, 2011.

53. Quoted in Emil Wilbekin. "Art Imitates Life." *Vibe*, September 2003, p. 150.

RECOMMENDED LISTENING

2Pac

*Me Against the World,** 1995

50 Cent

*Get Rich or Die Tryin',** 2003

A Tribe Called Quest

People's Instinctive Travels and the Paths of Rhythm, 1990

The Low End Theory, 1991

Beastie Boys

*Licensed to Ill,** 1986

Big Daddy Kane

Long Live the Kane, 1988

*It's a Big Daddy Thing,** 1989

Bone Thugs-N-Harmony

*Creepin on ah Come Up,** 1994

Boogie Down Productions

*Criminal Minded,** 1987

*By All Means Necessary,** 1988

Cypress Hill

*Cypress Hill,** 1991

De La Soul

*3 Feet High and Rising,** 1989

*De La Soul Is Dead,** 1991

D.J. Jazzy Jeff & the Fresh Prince

He's the DJ, I'm the Rapper, 1988

Dr. Dre

*The Chronic,** 1992

Eminem

*The Marshall Mathers LP,** 2000

On his second major-label album, the Detroit rapper takes rap storytelling to new heights, as evidenced on "Stan," his touching tale of a stalker fan. Much of the album's ferocious rhetoric has the potential to offend nearly anyone, but Eminem's lyrics are among the best in the genre.

EPMD

Strictly Business, 1988

Eric B. & Rakim

Paid In Full, 1987

The Fugees

*The Score,** 1996

Grandmaster Flash & the Furious Five

The Message, 1982

Ice Cube

*AmeriKKKa's Most Wanted,** 1990

*Death Certificate,** 1991

Jay-Z

*Vol. 2 . . . Hard Knock Life,** 1998

*The Blueprint,** 2001

*The Black Album,** 2003

Kanye West

*The College Dropout,** 2004

*Late Registration,** 2005

Lauryn Hill

The Miseducation of Lauryn Hill, 1998

LL Cool J

*Bigger and Deffer (BAD),** 1987

Lil Jon & the East Side Boyz

*Kings of Crunk,** 2002

On their fourth album, the pioneers of the ultra-rowdy, chant-heavy "crunk" rap subgenre—Lil Jon, Big Sam, and Lil Bo—deliver their strongest collection. With several guest artists (including Mystikal and Krayzie Bone), the album could easily come off as a compilation, but Lil Jon's thunderous beats and the crew's signature energy make every song sound distinctly their own. This raucous album is light on messages and heavy on fun.

Ludacris

*Back for the First Time,** 2000

This Atlanta rapper's music contains a rare combination of edge, muscle, and comedic flair.

MC Lyte

Lyte as a Rock, 1988

M.I.A.

Paper Planes, 2007

Missy Misdemeanor Elliott

*Supa Dupa Fly,** 1997

Nas

*Illmatic,** 1994

*God's Son,** 2002

For the second time in his career (the first being his debut release, 1994's *Illmatic*), Nas delivers a near-perfect album with his sixth studio collection, a set that showcases his poetic gifts, ones that allow him to eloquently comment on life, death, persecution, and hip-hop culture. He evokes legendary hip-hop storyteller Slick Rick on the landmark, inspirational "I Can" and revisits hip-hop's rugged, spare sonic roots on the muscular "Made You Look."

Nicki Minaj

Pink Friday, 2010

The Notorious B.I.G.

Ready to Die, 1994

N.W.A

Straight Outta Compton, 1988

Efil4Zaggin, 1991

OutKast

Southernplayalisticadillacmuzik, 1994

Aquemini, 1998

Stankonia, 2000

With their fourth album, the Atlanta duo of Dre and Big Boi push hip-hop's sonic boundary with a spaced-out, Parliament-influenced album. The pair's clever, rapid-fire rhymes cover everything from parties to women to societal ills.

Public Enemy

It Takes a Nation of Millions to Hold Us Back, 1988

Fear of a Black Planet, 1990

Puff Daddy & the Family

No Way Out, 1997

Queen Latifah, featuring Monie Love

Ladies First, 1989

Run-D.M.C.

Run-D.M.C., 1984

Raising Hell, 1986

Salt 'N Pepa

Hot, Cool & Vicious, 1986

Schoolly D

Saturday Night! The Album, 1987

Slick Rick

The Great Adventures of Slick Rick, 1988

Snoop Dogg

Doggystyle, 1993

Three 6 Mafia

Chpt. 2 "World Domination", 1997

Wu-Tang Clan

Enter the Wu-Tang (36 Chambers), 1993

* This work contains explicit lyrics and adult subject matter.

GLOSSARY

B-boying: Also known as break dancing. An energetic style of hip-hop dance that often includes exaggerated body movements and acrobatic moves, such as whirls.

beat boxing: The act of using the mouth to create percussion sounds that serve as a beat for someone else to rap or sing to.

bhangra: A type of dance music practiced by people from the Punjab region of South Asia that is traditionally performed during harvest festivals and weddings and is characterized by the beating of a large two-headed drum.

blaxploitation: A film genre that emerged in the early 1970s that included films made for urban black audiences and that featured primarily black casts and soundtracks with funk and soul music.

breaks: A portion of a song in which the music playing would be only percussion.

DJing: Playing records and performing in front of an audience.

garage: A style of English rap with faster and heavier drum patterns than those typical of American rap music.

gold record: A term used to indicate that a record company has shipped five hundred thousand or more copies of a particular album to record stores.

graffiti: Writings or drawings sprayed, scribbled, or scratched on a wall or other surface.

Grammy Award: An accolade given by the National Academy of Recording Arts and Sciences to recognize an outstanding achievement in a particular part of the music industry.

hip-hop: A culture encompassing four main components: rapping, DJing, graffiti art, and B-boying.

mastertones: A ringtone that has been encoded with a sampled audio format such as WMA or MP3.

MC: A person who raps or who speaks in front of a crowd; short for master of ceremonies.

measure: An amount of time in music defined by a given number of beats within a specific duration.

mixer: A device that DJs normally put between two turntables to manipulate a record on one turntable without having to reach over the other turntable while it is playing.

mixtapes: A collection of songs featuring a variety of music from different artists that were not intended to be put together. The songs are assembled by DJs and were originally put on cassette tapes and, later, CDs.

needle drop: A practice in which a DJ drops the needle on a record at exactly the point he wants the record to play without having to cue it up or listen to it.

platinum record: A term used to indicate that a record company has shipped 1 million or more copies of a particular album to record stores.

rap: A component of hip-hop culture and a genre of music in which artists recite words over music.

reggae: A music genre indigenous to Jamaica typified by distinguishable subsidiary beats.

reggaeton: An energetic hybrid of rap and reggae.

sampling: The act of taking short portions, or samples, of previously recorded material and using them for a new song.

scratching: A technique in which a DJ moves a record back and forth against the needle, creating a scratching sound.

ska: A style of up-tempo popular music having a prominent offbeat that originated in Jamaica.

tagging: The act of a graffiti artist writing his or her name or nickname on a wall, bench, or other surface.

trip-hop: An English form of hip-hop typified by a mixture of break beats and down-tempo electronic music.

turntable: An audio component that has a circular, revolving plate used to support a phonograph record as it is played.

Books

Dan Charnas. *The Big Payback: The History of the Business of Hip-Hop*. New York: New American Library, 2010. The evolution of the rap business is examined here.

Chuck D with Yusuf Jah. *Fight the Power: Rap, Race, and Reality*. New York: Delacorte Press, 1997. Chuck D's first book contains commentary from the Public Enemy leader about rap, race, and America.

Jasmine Guy. *Afeni Shakur: Evolution of a Revolutionary*. New York: Atria Books, 2004. Actress Jasmine Guy penned this biography on the mother of rap star 2Pac.

Jay-Z. *Decoded*. New York: Spiegel & Grau, 2010. *Decoded* offers a look at the rapper's music and his life as detailed through his song lyrics and additional commentary.

Tamara Palmer. *Country Fried Soul: Adventures in Dirty South Hip*Hop*. San Francisco: Backbeat Books, 2005. *Country Fried Soul* offers a look at the vibrant Southern rap scene.

Tricia Rose. *Black Noise*. Hanover, NH: Wesleyan University Press, 1994. This book, subtitled *Rap Music and Black Culture in Contemporary America*, takes a scholarly look at rap music and hip-hop culture.

Adam Sexton, ed. *Rap on Rap*. New York: Delta, 1995. This collection of articles and essays examines the positive and negative aspects of rap.

The RZA. *The Wu-Tang Manual*. New York: Riverhead Freestyle, 2005. This definitive guide looks into the world and culture of the Wu-Tang Clan.

Tupac Amaru Shakur. *The Rose That Grew from Concrete*. New York: MTV Books/Pocket Books, 1999. A collection of poems written by the rap star.

Websites

AllHipHop (www.allhiphop.com). This thorough website includes news, features, reviews, and often reliable rumors about what is going on in the rap world and in hip-hop culture.

BallerStatus (www.ballerstatus.com). This rap-centric site covers items of interest to the members of hip-hop culture, including music, fashion, politics, sports, and gaming.

HipHopDX (www.hiphopdx.com).

Rap news, music videos, streaming singles, album reviews, interviews, and editorials make up this extensive website.

The Original Hip-Hop Lyrics Archive (www.ohhla.com). This comprehensive website contains extensive lists of lyrics from hundreds of rappers.

INDEX

Cold Crush Brothers, 16
Combs, Sean (Puff Daddy, Diddy), 42,
   75–81, *76*, 78–80, 118
Common (artist), 28
Compton's Most Wanted, 63
Crazy Legs, 33
Cypress Hill, 63

D

Daz Dillinger, 64, 89
De La Soul, 50–52
Death Row Records, 71, 74–75, 78–81
Def American Records, 57
Def Jam Records, 50, 102, 103
Derek B, 96–97, 98
Dilated People's Evidence, 109
Disco Fever (nightclub), 24, *24*
Disorderlies (movie), 37
Dizzee Rascal, 97
DJ Clue?, 93
DJ Drama, 94
DJ Hollywood, 25
DJ Honda, 100
DJ Jazzy Jeff & the Fresh Prince, 52
DJ Kayslay, 94
DJ Kool Herc, 14–16, 18–20, 25
DJ Krush, 100
DJ Premier, 102
DJ Quik, 63
DJ Yella, 56, 57
DJing
   block parties and, 15, 25
   breaks and, 15–16, 20–21, *21*, 24, 31
   comeback in popularity, 93–95
   competitions, 11, 18–19
   description, 8, 12, 14–15
   female DJs, 44–45, 54–55
   MCs and, 22–23
   mixtapes and, 93–95
   needle drops and, 20–21
   radio shows and, 34
   rapping and, 10, 40, 91, 93–94

scratching and, 20, 22, 93–94
   television and, 95
Doug E. Fresh, 37, 47
Dr. Dre, 56–67, *64*, 74–75, 80–81, 94, 105
Dr. J, 34–35
Drake, 90
Dru Down, 89
Drugs, 45, 56, 57

E

E-40, 89
Eazy-E, 56–57, *58*, 62, 63, 67–75, *69*
8Ball & MJG, 83–84, 88
Electro-funk, 31
Eminem, 11, 86, *86*, 94, 105, 109–110
Entourage (TV program), 112
Epic Records, 71
Eric B., 35, 47

F

Fab Five Freddy, 37, 73
Fabolous, 46
Fantastic Romantic Freaks, 18
Fat Boys, 37, 39
Fat Joe, 67
Fatback Band, 25
50 cent, 10, 94–95, *94*, 105
Flashdance (movie), 33–34, 72
Flavor Flav, *49*, 50, 73
Foxy Brown, 114
Fresh Prince of Bel-Air (TV program), 73
Funk music, 9, 31, 92
Funk of Martin, 56
Funkmaster Flex, 93
Funky 4+1, 28
Funky Four, 18

G

G Unit, 94
Game (artist), 116–117, *117*

PICTURE CREDITS

Cover image: © Kzenon/Shutterstock.com

© A.J. Sisco/Corbis, 76

© Al Pereira/Michael Ochs Archives/Getty Images, 17, 61

© Anthony Barboza/Getty Images, 29

© Brian Cahn/Zuma Press/Corbis, 13

© Carl Posey/Corbis, 103

© Chad Batka/Corbis, 86, 114

© Chi Modu/Diverse Images/Corbis, 69, 79

© David Corio/Michael Ochs Archives/Getty Images, 45

© David Redfern/Redferns/Getty Images, 51

© Evan Agostini/Getty Images, 91

© Janette Beckman/Getty Images, 19, 36, 54

© Jared Milgrim/Corbis, 111

© Jeff Kravitz/FilmMagic, Inc./Getty Images, 65

© Jemal Countess/WireImage/Getty Images, 33

© Jerome Albertini/Corbis, 84

© KMazur/WireImage/Getty Images, 101

© Louise Wilson/WireImage/Getty Images, 117

© Mark Peterson/Corbis, 64

© Maury Phillips/WireImage/Getty Images, 88

© Michael Ochs Archives/Getty Images, 9, 26

© Moses Robinson/WireImage/Getty Images, 94

© Neal Preston/Corbis, 73

© Pam Springsteen/Corbis, 43

© Pascal Parrot/Sygma/Corbis, 98

© Raymond Boyd/Michael Ochs Archives/Getty Images, 58

© Robertus Pudyanto/Demotix/Corbis, 106

© Suzie Gibbons/Redferns/Getty Images, 49

© Ted Thai/Time & Life Pictures/Getty Images, 24

ABOUT THE AUTHOR

Soren Baker has had more than 2,300 articles published in such outlets as the *Los Angeles Times*, *Chicago Tribune*, *The Source*, and RedBullUSA.com. He's penned liner notes for albums by 2Pac, Ice Cube, and others, and has worked on television programs for VH1 and Fuse. He is the author of seven other books, including 2011's *I'm The White Guy—The Tech N9ne Edition* and *The Making of Game's The R.E.D. Album*, which he co-authored with Game.